The *Independent* Board Director

Selecting and Using the Best Non-Executive Directors to Benefit Your Business

David Clutterbuck and Peter Waine

McGRAW-HILL BOOK COMPANY

London · New York · St Louis · San Francisco · Auckland
Bogotá · Caracas · Lisbon · Madrid · Mexico · Milan
Montreal · New Delhi · Panama · Paris · San Juan · São Paulo
Singapore · Sydney · Tokyo · Toronto

Published by
McGRAW-HILL Book Company Europe
Shoppenhangers Road, Maidenhead, Berkshire, SL6 2QL, England
Telephone 0628 23432
Fax 0628 770224

British Library Cataloguing in Publication Data
Clutterbuck, David
Independent Board Director: Selecting and Using the Best Non-Executive
Directors to Benefit Your Business
I. Title   II. Waine, Peter
658.4

ISBN 0–07–707801–2

Library of Congress Cataloging-in-Publication Data
Clutterbuck, David.
The independent board director : selecting and using the best non-executive
directors to benefit your business / David Clutterbuck and Peter Waine.
    p.   cm.
Includes bibliographical references and index.
ISBN 0–07–707801–2
1. Directors of corporations.   I. Waine, Peter.   II. Title.
HD2745.C5   1993
658.4'22–dc20   93–24571   CIP

12345   CUP   97654

Typeset by Computape (Pickering) Ltd, North Yorkshire
and printed and bound at the University Press, Cambridge.

To Stephen Waine

Contents

Foreword

The independent *board director* makes a thoughtful and read-able contribution to the growing literature on corporate governance. The book is primarily concerned with the role of outside, independent directors on boards. I share the authors' aversion to the non-executive label; all else apart, this label is inaccurate because, at times that matter, the outside directors may have to act executively.

Leaving that aside, it is now generally accepted that boards gain from a combination of the breadth of view of outside directors and the depth of knowledge of the executive directors. Acceptance of the need for balance of that kind on a board clears the way for the next stage in the debate which centres on how to get the best out of a board made up in this way.

It is as well to recognize from the outset that this is a far from easy task, hence the frustrations expressed by both executive and outside directors in the pages which follow. There is hardly another field, however, in which companies could earn a more certain return than through modest improvements in the workings of their boards. *The* independent *board director* provides some useful pointers to ways in which boards could add more value to their companies—and to their members as well.

One of the reasons why boards, as we know them, do not always function as well as they might is that we ask them to undertake contrary, if not almost contradictory, duties. We expect them to be the driving force within an enterprise and at the same time to keep the business under prudent control, to be the accelerator and the brake. We require directors to be sufficiently knowledgeable about the workings of their companies to be answerable for their actions, while standing far enough back from their day-to-day management to retain their objectivity. We expect them to look inwards at the businesses for which they are responsible and outwards at their less well-defined responsibilities to society.

These tensions can be resolved constructively and are by successful boards. The right degree of tension within a board sparks debate and ensures that the best available options are surfaced, rather than those which may have been first proposed. It is primarily the job of the chairman to maintain the balance between too much argument and too little. As the authors say, 'Getting the balance of creative, positive conflict right is one of the chairman's most difficult tasks.'

That particular balance is achieved in the first place by drawing board members, both from those who understand the business in detail and whose livelihood depends upon it, and from those whose experience lies primarily outside the business and who are independent of it in a material sense. The first group have the power which comes from knowledge and ready access to information, while the power of the second group depends on their ability to influence. For the two groups to work effectively together, each has to value the contribution of the other.

A second aspect of balance is between personalities and backgrounds. Here there is a need for board members to 'fit', but perhaps not to fit too comfortably. Board members have to feel that they have enough in common to be able to work together and to arrive at a broadly agreed view, but not so much in common that they start with the same view. I strongly support the authors' call for boards to tap 'a wider pool of expertise' and to avoid 'the depressing uniformity of background' of board members which is still too common.

While executive directors of similar standing from other companies may provide a board with a solid base, there is a strong case for a leavening of directors from different backgrounds with experience in the private and public sectors. This has the advantage of broadening the points of view around the board table and avoids the outside directors being too close in their mindset to the executive directors. More importantly it recognizes that today's boards spend less time than they once did looking inwards at the running of their businesses and more time looking outwards at the changing environment in which their businesses operate.

There are two further reasons for looking more widely than at other executives when building a board team. One is that it brings in more able women candidates, few of whom as yet are on the boards of public limited companies, but many of whom are holding equivalent positions of considerable authority in the public sector, in voluntary organizations and in the professions. Another is that a less limited view of what constitutes relevant board experience will help to allay concerns about the demand for competent outside directors outrunning the supply.

But balancing the board is not simply a question of having the right proportions of insiders and outsiders, with the outsiders not replicating the insiders too closely. It also turns, as the authors stress, on enough of the outside directors being independent and on the board as a whole, outsiders and insiders, working together. All of which means that the key to an effective board lies in the way in which its members are chosen.

The nomination process needs to start with an assessment of what new infusion of experience and personality would be most likely to benefit the existing board. In some ways the search for a new outside director is more difficult than for a new senior executive and hence justifies at least as much care and thought. With executives their past attainments are a good guide to their future performance. The choice of an outside director has to be based more on judgement, because there is less in the way of an established track record to go on.

Equally, it is hard to judge in advance how potential outside directors will interact with their other board colleagues. Personality is arguably more of a factor when the role turns on the ability to listen, to influence and to persuade, than when it entails responsibility for action within a defined executive structure.

The majority of outside directors on the board of a publicly quoted company should be both independent and able to add value to the board they have joined. This leads to a number of conclusions. The first, which has already been touched on, is that the search for a new outside director has to be at least as thorough as for any other senior appointment. It should start with as clear a profile of the kind of person being sought as possible.

Second, as with an executive appointment, it helps to have a choice of candidates who seem to answer the board's needs. An element of competition ensures that the best appointment will be made, not simply an uncontroversial one.

Third, the board as a whole should be involved in determining the nature of the gap to be filled on the board and in the ultimate choice of who is to be put forward to fill it. This is as true of executive as it is of outside board appointments. The board needs to be fully involved, partly because the board team has to work together, but more fundamentally because their involvement strengthens the independence of the outside directors.

Directors who owe their place on a board, or feel that they do, to the chairman or chief executive have their independence compromised to that extent from the outset. Patronage undermines independence. On the other hand, directors who have been selected in competition with others through a formal board process of nomination have the confidence of being appointed on their merits and the independence which goes with it.

Independence is largely a matter of character, although sensible guidance on what constitutes independence is set out in *The independent board director*. Independence of judgement and the courage to stand their ground are the personal qualities which I look for in outside directors. Those qualities come particularly into play when the interests of the executive directors and those of the company could diverge, for example over a takeover bid, top management succession, or directors' pay and in carrying out that most difficult of board tasks assessing the performance of the company and of the executives.

Good selection deserves to be matched by good induction. The degree of care which companies take to explain what they expect of their directors is a measure of the value which they place on them.

What role have shareholders in ensuring that the companies in which they have invested have balanced boards? In the textbook corporate governance model, the shareholders appoint the directors and replace them if they lose confidence in their conduct of the business. The reality is different. Yet it is difficult to see how to involve shareholders directly in the nomination process, without a properly constituted shareholders' committee representing both individual and institutional shareholders. This would require these two groups to work together in a way we have not yet seen. Shareholders, small and large, are however fully entitled to put forward their views on the way in which their boards should be made up.

All shareholders have a positive part to play in bringing about better balanced boards by encouraging their companies to explain the process by which potential directors are selected and the contribution which board members make to the governance of the company. The more open the system by which board members are chosen and the clearer the explanation of how individual boards go about their work, the better placed will be the shareholders to comment, question and influence the outcome. One aim which all classes of shareholder should hold in common is that of raising the standards of governance in their companies.

A means to that end is a balanced board. It is the haphazard way in which too many boards of directors are still formed that makes the message of *The* independent *board director* so important.

Adrian Cadbury

Preface

There are some 8000 non-executive or independent directors (NEDs) of private sector companies in the United Kingdom, plus at least half as many people holding similar positions directing the fortunes of public sector bodies and voluntary organizations. Many of them make an excellent, substantial contribution to the health and growth of the boards, on which they sit. Many do not. Many companies, which have independent directors, are unclear about the benefits they expect from them.

It is only recently that non-executive directors have come under serious scrutiny from the press and business academia. So it is not surprising that relatively little is known about the shadowy world of the NED, especially when—by their very nature—board meetings are normally closed events.

In an attempt to present a practical guide to best practice we have brought together in this book what state of the art knowledge there is, including the results of a detailed survey and interviews we have carried out ourselves. Many of our conclusions question conventional wisdom. If you are a chairman looking for suitable NEDs, or an experienced director with a conviction that your talents could help other companies, then you will at the very least find some food for thought in the following pages.

Underlying our arguments is an unashamed assumption that NEDs are generally 'a good thing'. Our own observations certainly support the view that effective NEDs can be a major positive force in most corporate environments. In particular, they bring a much-needed balance, an exposure to alternative views that moderate excesses of enthusiasm (or pessimism) among the executive team. Sadly, those companies where NEDs can often be of most use—smaller companies, which often lack the depth and breadth of management expertise to avoid sometimes obvious mistakes—are those least likely to have them. Equally sadly, the evidence suggests that even organizations, which do have NEDs, often either appoint the wrong people for the wrong reasons, or fail to make proper use of them. It is not surprising then, that NEDs are often unsure of what is expected of them, or what their role on a particular board should be.

Being a non-executive director offers good career development, and is a crucial prerequisite to becoming a future chairman or a chief executive because it broadens the candidate's corporate experience.

Our aim is to heighten awareness of the NED role, so that more companies take advantage of it, and to help companies improve the way in which they select and use NEDs. We also hope to encourage a broader spectrum of suitably qualified people to put themselves forward as NEDs. We are sanguine enough to recognize that NEDs will not provide a panacea for poor executive management—and nor should they—but we do believe that if every company of more than a dozen employees were to have genuinely independent, regular advice at board level, the very high rate of business failures of the early 1990s could have been sharply reduced.

David Clutterbuck
Peter Waine

Acknowledgements

The authors would like to acknowledge the co-operation and assistance of all those who contributed anecdotal material to this book. In particular, we are indebted to:

Sir Adrian Cadbury, Barry Dinan, Denise Maher, Clare Hogg, Keith Carby, Kep Simpson and Colin Coulson-Thomas.

1 So what is a non-executive director?

Ask the man in the street to describe an independent or non-executive director and he would probably say something along the lines of: 'a friend of the chairman; someone who lends his or her name to the company without having to work there'.

Ask a trade union official and the response might be along the lines of: 'someone on the old boy network, probably retired, supplementing a pension'.

A lawyer might say; 'the same as an executive director, only usually with less knowledge of what is going on'.

A broker might be more cynical, describing independent directors as 'the people who should fire lousy executives on the shareholders' behalf, but rarely do'.

The fact is that few people, including many of the companies that have independent directors and many independent directors themselves, have more than a partial picture of the roles and responsibilities of the job. Moreover, what publicity is given to these subjects tends to be negative, particularly in the scandal-ridden early 1990s. What were the independent directors of the Maxwell companies doing while the chairman embezzled hundreds of millions? How did the independent directors of Burton Group plc allow the executives to award themselves such remarkably generous incentive bonus schemes? Why did the independent directors of BCCI not know what was happening? All these are legitimate questions, asked vociferously by both the press and Members of Parliament.

Did the fault—if fault there was—lie with the individuals, with the concept of independent directors, or with the way the independent directors were used? Are we expecting too much of independent directors? Or does the way they are appointed mean that the independent view is more myth than reality? It is inevitable that these issues should surface and they have occupied much of the time of the Cadbury Committee on Corporate Governance; but in order to draw real conclusions, it is essential to know more about independent directors themselves. Clearly, it is not always easy to decide between standing up and making a fuss and attempting to influence the executives through quiet reasoning—especially when there is so little practical guidance for independent directors. It is perhaps not surprising that independent directors do not always find it easy to know when to raise their heads above the parapet, or stand up and be counted. Many intelligent and successful business people allow incompetent boards to continue to operate and misbehave under their very noses.

What research there is on independent directors lends support to the view that all aspects of the job—selection, induction, definition of roles, remuneration, the maintenance of independence, length of service, how to deal with conflicts of interest and so on—tend to be handled in an amateurish manner across a wide spectrum of British industry and commerce. A 1991 study by management consultants PA[1] found that 70 per cent of independent director appointments were personal acquaintances of the chairman or another board member. Our own survey[2] was very much in line with this result, at approximately 60 per cent, with rather more than half of these approached directly by the chief executive. Regrettably, such appointments frequently lack the rigour of executive appointments, while at the same time they undermine the most important element of the independent director's contribution—that of truly independent advice. This situation could be drastically improved if greater emphasis were placed on the concept of independence.

WHAT DO WE MEAN BY 'INDEPENDENT'?

True independence takes two main forms—of thought and of obligation. The independent director needs both to be and to be seen to be his or her own person.

Independence of thought demands that the director is able to bring a different perspective to strategic discussions; that he or she is not so much of a confidant(e) to the executives as to become uncritical. From this point of view, close personal friendship with the chairman or chief executive may be a significant reason for not accepting the role.

Independence of obligation demands that the director should have no possible conflict of interest. In its campaign to force companies, in which it invests, to appoint a majority of independent directors the New York Common Retirement Fund published a useful list of characteristics to avoid. A director cannot be considered independent, it declared, if he or she:

- has been employed by the company or an affiliate company in an executive capacity during the previous three years;
- is a paid adviser or consultant to the company or its affiliates;
- is employed by a major customer or supplier;
- has a personal service contract with the company;
- is related to an executive director.

THE INDEPENDENT DIRECTOR AND THE SHAREHOLDERS

In theory, an independent director is appointed to represent the interests of the shareholders. In practice, the effective independent director will balance the interests of all stakeholders. Independence in this context means not getting trapped into the attitudes, values and short-term objectives of the executive team.

The Institutional Shareholders Committee's (ISC)[3] code of practice for independent directors places an obligation on them to report to the ISC if they are unhappy with the performance of the executive directors. However, as executives such as John Napier of WH Smith pointed out when the code was announced in 1991, individual executives are equally obliged to report to shareholders if they have serious concerns about the way the company is being managed.

If the independent directors are in the majority, they should take action on their own account and will no doubt explain why to shareholders. The problem of who to consult arises only when the independent directors are in a voting minority, or are split about the appropriate action to take.

WHAT ARE INDEPENDENT DIRECTORS FOR?

Depending on who you ask, independent directors are either extremely valuable or at best an unnecessary drain on company resources. In a survey carried out by the venture capital organization 3i[4] before the publication of the draft Cadbury report on corporate governance, 95 per cent of finance directors said that independent directors did not make a crucial contribution to shareholder value and 31 per cent said independent directors were not really important. Another survey, this time by PRO NED,[5] found that while 62 per cent of chairmen thought independent directors to be very effective, only 37 per cent of chief executives held the same view. Among auditors and institutional shareholders, only 3 per cent considered that independent directors made a significant contribution.

The Cadbury Committee made a number of recommendations,[6] which reinforced the importance of having independent directors (it felt, as do the authors and many other observers, that the term non-executive director is somewhat misleading). The main recommendations included the following:

- All boards of public companies should have independent directors.
- Audit committees should be wholly composed of independent directors.
- Compensation committees should be 'wholly or mainly' composed of independent directors.

- The roles of chairman and chief executive should be divided; normally the chairman should be independent.

The recommendations drew a fair amount of flak, however, notably from Sir Owen Green, chairman of BTR. While he recognizes that independent directors 'add a bit more objectivity and a bit less subjectivity to board discussions', he does not agree that companies should be compelled to have them. He points out that '90 per cent of all recent corporate failures will have had non-executive directors on their boards' and asks: 'Where's the evidence that they could have fulfilled the role Cadbury wants for them? Does the [Cadbury] committee think this will prevent other scandals, other failures?'

So on the one hand we apparently have Cadbury and chairmen (many of them, being independent directors themselves perhaps having at least a little self-interest in their enthusiasm) arguing strongly for independent directors; and external observers taking a rather more sanguine and less favourable view. In practice, each of these opinions is correct—at the individual level. If a company is clear about what it wants its independent directors to do; if it is rigorous in its selection procedures; and if it is disciplined in how it makes use of the independent minds it employs—then there is ample evidence that major benefits flow.

If, on the other hand, the company is not prepared to make full and proper use of its independent directors (for example, if like Robert Maxwell the chairman only wishes to use independent directors as a screen of respectability), or if appointments are made haphazardly, then no amount of legislation or Stock Exchange rules will allow these people to contribute meaningfully or to protect stakeholders' interests.

One of the results of Cadbury is undoubtedly an increase in the number of companies that have independent directors for their own sake—as a relatively low-cost concession to the Stock Exchange and public opinion. There will also probably always be companies that use independent directorships as rewards for long service or political favours. Equally, however, we expect there to be an increasing number of companies that recognize the value of an independent voice at the top and are prepared to make effective use of it.

WHY DO COMPANIES NEED INDEPENDENT DIRECTORS?

There is no legal requirement for a company to have any independent directors, let alone specific requirements on the executive/non-executive composition of the board. Some organizations, such as many of the building societies, have traditionally operated with a board made up almost exclusively of independent directors. Others have none at all.

Among the likely impacts of European integration is a requirement for some form of supervisory direction of the executive team. While the United Kingdom is unlikely to adopt the German/Scandinavian model of separate supervisory boards, a formal representation of independent directors may well become obligatory for publicly quoted companies.

The current trend, however, particularly among quoted companies, is to increase the number of independent directors. A 1990 study by Korn/Ferry International[7] found that, while for most of the 1980s, independent directors occupied about one-third of all seats in quoted company boardrooms, by 1989 the proportion had risen to 44 per cent (50 per cent in companies with sales over £500 million). To some extent, this is a reaction to financial scandals, but it represents a general trend to increase the number of independent voices on public boards. Not surprisingly, this rapid increase has given rise to questions about whether there are really that many suitable people available, and if so, whether the most suitable people have been selected.

There is also an increasing emphasis on choosing independent directors on the basis of genuine contribution. Charles Batchelor, writing in *The Financial Times* (20 March 1990)[8] puts it succinctly:

> The days when companies appointed non-executive directors for their titles and the glitter they gave to the letterhead may not be completely dead. But a new realism entered into the choice of non-executives in the 1980s and they are now expected to deliver real value for money. This trend was encouraged by legislation, which has made it less easy for non-executives to avoid their responsibilities if anything goes wrong.

The reasons for using independent directors vary considerably and are frequently complex. The most common reasons are described below.

To provide an outside view; to challenge introverted thinking

It is very easy for top management to become locked into a distorted view of the world, making assumptions about future business trends that are ill-founded or over-optimistic. A good independent director can help the top team recognize warning signs in the figures and in the market. He or she can also alert the executives to potential competition and to the impact of business cycles. Arguably, one of the reasons Bovis maintained its profitability during the 1991–92 recession, while almost every other construction and property company ran into severe difficulties, was because the independent directors exhorted the executives to take heed of the 10–12 year UK cycle of the UK property business. Bovis directed investment into developing overseas markets at a time when other companies decided they had too much business at home to divert executive attention into international adventures.

A more mundane example comes from Clive Bastin, ex-managing partner of Spicer & Pegler and a serving non-executive director on a number of boards:

> I was able to persuade a board to take a second opinion on a major litigation issue involving many millions of pounds simply because all the directors were seeking to back the colleague in litigation rather than looking at the issue objectively. The executives, in short, were getting too emotionally involved and not looking at the potential compromise which needed to be aired.

An effective independent director, not being locked into the everyday problems of the organization, is able to step back and see issues from a different perspective. He or she is able to ask apparently naïve questions, question assumptions and relate situations to similar events personally encountered elsewhere. This person is also able to take a longer time horizon, asking questions such as: 'Will this product still be the technology leader in three years' time?'; or 'If you intend to sell within five years, how specifically are you going to maximize the value of the company between now and that time?'

The value of informed *naïveté* is not necessarily that it introduces remarkable new ideas or insights, but that it helps executives face up to what they probably already knew, instinctively. It may be particularly valuable in the company that is doing well, as opposed to the company in trouble, because executives in the former can easily become complacent.

Areas where, in our experience, informed *naïveté* has particular impact include long-range planning, determining executive roles, management structures and business focus.

Typical of the smaller company requiring an independent director is a family company, Yates Brothers, quoted in a 1989 article in *The Director*.[9] Established in Manchester over 100 years ago as a port importer, it is now chaired by the founder's grandson Christopher Martin-Bird, and operates some 40 wine bars in the North of England. Rapid growth, both organic and through acquisition, marked the 1980s. While the company had a succession of independent directors from the family, it used the opportunity presented by the retirement of twin brothers to bring in some independent directors from outside, who would bring fresh ideas and perceptions. Explained Martin-Bird: 'As a family business, we definitely needed comments from outside the company. Family members tend not to be as objective as they need to be.'

On the other side of the coin, executives of family firms often make very good non-executives—family members often receive years of informal training for the job.

One reason why executives often do not present different views is that they are afraid of the chairman. According to Gordon Owen, former group chief executive of Cable and Wireless plc: 'It's difficult to disagree with the chairman if you are an executive director. Their job and career is at stake. They are only human. The independent director can argue and disagree. He is in a much stronger position—but effectively only if he is not solely a chairman's appointment in the first place.'

Clive Bastin agrees:

> A key role of an independent director is to challenge thinking on future strategy. My own experience of doing just that suggests that if the non-executive chairman and the chief executive do not want to change their thinking then an independent director working with his other independent directors has little chance of changing opinion, especially if the company is still successful. The other executive directors are often too frightened of their own position to stand up to the chairman and chief executive especially in times of recession.

To control the chairman/chief executive

When a company has an entrepreneur at the helm, it helps to have a moderating influence to bring him or her down to earth. The independent directors can keep an eye on the chairman's morals, opinion, hobby-horses—especially if he or she is on the acquisition path, is very strong willed and/or is acting as CEO, too. Typical exercises by the chairman that need to be identified and restrained include:

- Confusing own cheque book with the company's.
- Using company money to buy honours.
- Making major commitments, especially to 'grand' projects.

Stephen Hayklan, former chairman of Wiggins Group, provides an example of the latter:

> I serve as non-executive deputy chairman in a company involved with sponsorship of theatre productions, and whilst I like the theatre very much, I could in no way be classed as an expert. However, it probably falls to me to curb the enthusiasm of the amateur experts in theatre who would like to back pretty well every production which is put forward to the board, with potentially disastrous results. This is particularly true of the executive directors who are also producer directors in the company, who seem to think that balancing the books is pretty irrelevant.

That said, the independent director is not there to restrain entrepreneurial spirit—'his or her foot is on the accelerator, not the brake' as one prominent industrialist expresses it.

It might be said that recent examples indicate the manifest failure of independent directors to exert real control of over-powerful chief executives. It is not uncommon to hear comments such as that of one investor at BET's 1992 annual general meeting, complaining at the high debt level and reduced profits resulting from acquisitions in the 1980s: 'five non-executive directors have been on the board since at least 1987 ... Surely they must have known? Why haven't they resigned?' The volume of applause indicated that he was not alone in his opinion.

Similar angry comments were made concerning the Maxwell directors. But in fact the actions of the independent directors may actually have helped force the exposure of wrongdoing. According to *The Daily Telegraph*,[10] at the September meeting of the main board, independent directors Sir Robert Clark and Alan Clements asked for a great deal more information about finance and critical operational issues such as circulation figures for Mirror Group newspapers. Clark demanded an explanation of the balance sheet each board meeting, and for details of all changes in the holdings of investors who held more than 1 million shares. It is doubtful whether Robert Maxwell could have continued to maintain the subterfuge of his share and pension dealings under such scrutiny—although no doubt he would have tried!

Similarly, though the independent directors of business failed to prevent the excesses of Ernest Saunders, several of them proved their worth subsequently by guiding the company through its most critical times while the management was overhauled.

In the United States, where 69 per cent of directors are non-executive and most public companies have a majority of independent directors on their boards, there is similar concern at how ineffectual independent directors can be. Jay Lorsch, of Harvard Business School and a colleague, Elizabeth McIver, carried out a survey of nearly 1000 independent directors. The results, published in a book, *Pawns or Potentates: The Reality of American's Corporate Boards*,[11] were summarized by *The Financial Times* as follows:

> Many boards, they say, are ineffective and under the thumb of powerful chief executives; they lack the power and sense of common purpose needed to oversee their companies as they should. Important issues are not discussed openly, or sufficiently quickly, and small management problems fester and tend to grow into crisis ...
>
> The most obvious restraint on outside directors is the entrenched power of the very person they are meant to be governing: the chief executive, who, in 80 per cent of US companies is also the chairman and thus controls the agenda of board meetings, decides what information is received in advance, and leads discussions in the boardroom.

To replace entrepreneurial flair

Particularly in the smaller company, when the entrepreneur sells up or dies, he or she is succeeded by managers rather than leaders. The company needs vision, enthusiasm and drive—none of which is likely to come from the management team, who are equally unlikely to put in over their heads a full time CEO, who does have those qualities. An independent director, on the other hand, especially acting in the chairman role, poses no threat and can be welcomed as a positive influence—as a sort of constitutional monarch, who sets the tone for the company and enables the managers to gel together as a team rather than waste energy on internecine politics.

Says Hayklan: 'Independent directors have been able to successfully embarrass executives into looking at new markets, particularly overseas, when the easy option for the executive directors is to do only what they have done before.'

To provide an international perspective

Few UK companies have appointed international advisory boards. But the need at one level for strategic level international input, and at another for cultural insights, still needs to be met in some form. Appointing international independent directors creates a whole new dimension for board discussions and helps avoid some of the catastrophes that occur, when all-UK boards make decisions about ventures overseas. The capacity for misunderstanding between business cultures is immense.

The contribution made by international directors can cover a whole variety of issues, from appropriate executive compensation packages to government negotiations.

The Korn/Ferry study[7] of UK boards of directors concludes that the ability to understand overseas markets and manage international relationships is now a basic requirement for the leaders of the UK's largest corporations. It is a requirement, however, not reflected in the current composition of UK boards. For example, 84 per cent of directors speak no foreign languages, and only 2 per cent speak more than two. Only 4 per cent of directors are foreign nationals, less than one-third of them being continental Europeans (the rest are mostly North Americans, Australians, or Irish). The proportion of those speaking no foreign languages was the same (84 per cent) for companies that generated more than half their turnover overseas; and at least two-thirds of the directors of these companies had never lived overseas. Only 7.5 per cent had experience of Western Europe (as opposed to 6 per cent for all companies).

Against this background some companies shine. Reckitt & Colman is one example. 'It's our policy to encourage the development of an international cadre of management. The executive directors we have at the moment represent the apex of a situation which began several years back,' explains Sir Michael Colman, Reckitt & Colman's chairman. Every one of the executive directors has considerable overseas experience, and most speak one or two foreign languages fluently. So far only one, Lalith de Mel, is a foreigner himself. However, his promotion is an indication of an underlying trend. At the next layer down there are Frenchmen, South Americans, New Zealanders and Americans. The French operation is run by a Swiss and the Benelux operation by a Greek. Reckitt & Colman in France is growing so fast, and so many 'high-flyers' in the company happen to be French, that

Sir Michael sees a French board member as a natural progression. Nevertheless, he is adamant that 'nationality is not a factor, we are committed to appoint the people with the greatest ability'. What is critical is their outlook. 'We all believe that no English person without international experience can be relied upon to open his eyes sufficiently to understand the competition.'

This approach is heartily endorsed by Leslie Dighton, founder and chairman of Corporate Renewal Associates, a consultancy that specializes in helping organizations reposition themselves. 'What you don't want on boards are representative directors of anything, geographical or functional, the only exception being the finance director. What you do need are people with the personal characteristics and qualities to allow them to make a genuine corporate contribution.'

Jean-Claude Larreche, Professor of Marketing at INSEAD, is a particularly interesting example of a foreign non-executive director. Sir Michael Colman is enthusiastic about the value of Larreche's wide-ranging experience: 'He points out how others have tackled a problem to enable us to miss out a step ... he frequently opens our eyes.' But it is his knowledge and experience as a professor and consultant that is valued, rather than his particular viewpoint as a French resident.

United Biscuits also includes foreign non-executives on its board. Unlike Reckitt & Colman, 20 years ago United Biscuits had no overseas interests. Today, 47 per cent of the company's revenue comes from outside the United Kingdom. 'We've been quite big in the US for some time, about 15 years,' explains Robert Clarke, chairman of United Biscuits, and correspondingly the board includes both executive and non-executive American directors.

Now the company aims to increase sales in Europe. 'If we are going to expand, then we need to have people who think internationally,' reasons Clarke. 'Nationals understand how things work in their countries—we are not expecting them to come up with ideas. We need to know how people think, and how things work.' To that end, Clarke has recently appointed a Dutchman and a German, Ray van Schaik, chairman of the

executive board of Heineken, and Thorlef Spickschen, chairman of the executive board of Boehringer Mannheim, as
non-executive directors.

They have not been chosen for their specific knowledge of
Holland or Germany. 'What is required', comments Michael
Brandon, a partner at Korn/Ferry, 'is someone with a view of
the world, but from another mountain'. As a professor of a
European (as opposed to French) business school, Larreche,
says Brandon, is an excellent example . Pehr Gyllenhammar,
executive chairman of Volvo AB, and chairman of the board
of Procordia AB appears to be another example; he is on the
board of Pearson plc, Reuters Holdings plc, United Tech-
nologies Corporation, Kissengers Associates, NV Philips'
Gloeilampenfabrieken and Renault SA. Brandon is confident
that such people can be easily found (although he warns
against non-executives who are too high powered to find the
time to attend board meetings).

Dighton is less convinced:

> I think there is a real conundrum here. If a non-executive director
> is there for a special purpose, does this not clash with the primary
> role of custodian of corporate wellbeing, as part of a two-tier
> board in-waiting? ... People like Wyman [the non-executive US
> director on United Biscuit's board] and Gyllenhammar under-
> stand this role; they are carrying it out in their own companies.
> But those with an uncommon culture and language may not.

Those who can combine an international viewpoint with
their principal role as a director are rare. Those companies
which cannot harness such individuals will have to find other
ways to ensure that their strategy remains sensitive to global
markets. Diluting the strength of the board to fulfil its initial
role is not the solution.

At BAA, for example, says chairman Dr Brian Smith:

> We are a very British organisation trading in many parts of the
> world. We needed to bring in wider international experience on
> the board. How you do that is by appointing the right indepen-
> dent director. We chose Sir Patrick Wright, the former head of the
> Diplomatic Service. He is a very intelligent man with plenty of
> international experience. It has to be said, too, that a modern

British ambassador is also a commercial animal, with a great deal of experience at establishing trade links.

BOC and ICI, too, have a history of appointing international independent directors to encourage a more global perspective in strategy-making. Says a spokesman for ICI:

> ICI is an international company operating in all areas of the world. Key growth areas for the company are the USA, Europe and Asia Pacific, and advice from our non-executive directors from countries within these areas is invaluable for ICI's board deliberations.
>
> Equally, the views of the non-executive directors from abroad on how the economies of their own regions are operating is immensely useful for ICI.

To steer the company through a difficult or sensitive transition

When Steve Shirley, founder of FI Group, wanted to deliver control of the company into the hands of its employees and associates, she turned to Sir Peter Thompson, former chairman of National Freight Consortium. Thompson's experience in managing NFC's transition from public ownership to employee ownership was invaluable.

Kep Simpson, a consultant and independent director of several small and medium-sized companies, provides another example:

> A medium-sized consumer durables company on whose board I sit has a problem that the two long-serving independent directors are retiring and they have a mishmash of executives, who are not necessarily suitable as directors. Part of my role as a new non-executive director is to help them sort out what to do. But I have had to make it clear that only they can actually make it happen.

A similar role, whether as chairman or simply as another independent director, can be valuable in many other transition stages, such as going public (or private), taking in loan capital, changing from one generation at the helm to the next, or simply through an expected period of rapid growth.

One of the most critical transition periods is when the company is up for sale. For example, the entrepreneur selling his or her business to a larger company will be pulled in several directions at once. On the one hand, there is the need to devote as much time as possible to the business, to ensure that it is in peak condition at the time of sale (particularly if there is to be an earn-out clause), so the entrepreneur cannot afford to take his or her eye off the ball. On the other hand, the complexities of selling a business are extremely time-consuming, especially for someone with little previous experience. The ideal solution is to appoint an independent director who has sold companies before, to handle the negotiations, while the entrepreneur concentrates on adding value to the company.

Another critical transition is post-acquisition, especially in merger situations. Again, the right independent director can help ease the conflicts that inevitably result as two teams of managers jockey for position. Where two national cultures are brought together, the potential clashes can be even worse. An independent director with experience of working in both cultures can help pinpoint potential troublespots early on.

In another example of transitional management, John Allan, executive main board director at BET, was an independent director of a company which used to be independent but now belongs to a larger group. From his experience, he says independent directors can make an invaluable contribution in such instances.

The transition between small and medium-sized business is a much longer drawn out affair, and full of pitfalls. Patient, worldly-wise independent directors—particularly those who have managed this transition in their own companies—can be essential members of the team. Given the chronic shortage of middle-sized companies in the United Kingdom, the authors believe strongly that there should be greater encouragement from the Department of Trade and Industry (DTI), from the Confederation of British Industry and elsewhere, for the growth-oriented small company to appoint independent directors. Even an organization of only a dozen or so people can find the relationship extremely valuable.

To improve the board processes

Says Sir Nigel Mobbs, chairman of Slough Estates: 'A good non-executive director and his other non-executive director colleagues will bring a degree of discipline to a board in the way in which they report, analyse and determine decisions.'

To bring specialist knowledge

Independent directors have been appointed because of their special experience and know-how in topics as diverse as handling large-scale redundancy programmes, setting up share option schemes, or arranging international loans. As we have already indicated, the board should be clear at the start whether or not this input would best come from board membership or from some other form of association. A good rule of thumb can be how long the specialist knowledge is needed at a strategic or policy level. If it is for less than two years, then it is probably inappropriate to offer an independent director post.

One increasingly popular form of specialist independent director is the overseas executive, appointed because of personal knowledge of business conditions and opportunities in his or her home country. There are also a few (very few) genuinely international executives, who can bring a useful overview of global strategies to the more localized decision-making of UK boards.

Another valuable specialist for some boards is the public relations expert. Although people from this background with boardroom competence are few and far between, the management of the organization's public reputation is all too easily neglected as a board agenda item.

Neglected internal departments can also receive a much-needed boost in status by the appointment of an independent director from the same discipline. The information technology department, for example, often reports through accounting; training through personnel. If there is no sensible route to give these functions direct boardroom access through executive directors, then a suitable independent director may provide a viable solution.

To provide continuity

Where the CEO is appointed for five years or less, there is a tendency for organizations to go through wild swings of policy much on the lines of those that happen when a new government of a different party takes office. While the independent director should not be there to obstruct change, he or she should help the new CEO retain the best of the predecessor's policies, while encouraging the best of the new ideas. The less an independent director is perceived to have been 'owned' by the former CEO, the more likely the new CEO is to turn to him or her for information and support as he or she grows into the job.

To help identify alliances and acquisitions

An independent director with a strong network can be invaluable in finding targets and opening negotiations.

To help maintain an ethical climate

The requirement for boards to be seen to be ethical and socially responsible is becoming increasingly important. Pressure from ethical investment funds, from public pressure groups and from consumers is all combining to push ethical considerations up the boardroom agenda. At the same time, there is a steady rise in the risk of prosecution, to which directors are exposed if the company does neglect its responsibilities in respect of environmental protection, health and safety, or equal opportunities, for example. As Dr Brian Smith puts it:

> The independent directors have a responsibility for the cleanliness of the company. These days, the excuse that you did not know is no longer good enough I'm afraid. This is an aspect of the independent director that is becoming more and more important. The Great and the Good idea of independent directors is gone. A genuine monitoring role for the quality of the company is now expected of independent directors by the shareholders.

Occasionally, companies appoint independent directors specifically for their understanding of these issues. Some US companies also have ethics committees, of which the majority of members are independent directors. An extension of the concept, developed in the United States, is to give a particular independent director responsibility for monitoring ethical behaviour in the organization. One of the benefits of this approach is that employees, who believe the company is acting illegally or immorally, but who cannot gain a hearing through the formal executive management structure, have a clearly recognizable alternative, where they can make their case. Companies using this approach claim that it reduces the likelihood of whistleblowing, with all its risks of damage to the company's reputation, and that encouraging constructive dissent promotes a healthier corporate climate overall.

As a confidant(e) to the chief executive/chairman

It is a truism that it is lonely at the top. The CEO or executive chairman often has few people to turn to for an honest answer, who are at a peer level and understand the kinds of problem and pressure being faced. The other executive directors, no matter how supportive and loyal they may be, cannot normally fulfil this role.

CarnaudMetalbox's David O'Shaugnessy points up the essential dilemma in this role: 'It's important to distinguish between a confidant and a close incestuous friend. Managing relationships is a critical skill of an independent director.' Indeed, says Sir Anthony Gill of Lucas, if an independent director gets so closely associated with the chairman or chief executive that he or she fails to challenge, then this is a sign that the independent director's usefulness has reached its end.

To interface with key external audiences

Many executive managers—especially action-oriented visionaries—find it difficult to deal with professionals such as lawyers and accountants, who will not give them the straight, unequivocal answers they demand. The experienced independent director can come between the CEO and these professionals at critical times, providing a useful buffer. However, he or she must avoid the danger of absorbing an executive role, or of becoming the sole source of information to the CEO on these topics.

At the same time, independent directors often have the contacts and experience to get the maximum benefit from relationships with key external audiences including influential trade associations and professional bodies. As George Novelli, deputy managing director of Mercury Communications puts it: 'A company needs to be advised correctly when dealing with professional bodies. The non-executive director can help here. It is not just a question of ethics but of generating respect.'

To bring women into the organization at the top

Most companies have a dearth of senior women managers ready and able to advance to board positions. Yet the benefits of having a visible cadre of female executives are considerable. They can, for example, provide a strong role model for younger women in the organization, and they can be a useful demonstration of the company's commitment to equal opportunities. (Some companies even use female independent directors directly on the university milkround for just this purpose.) The difficulties lie firstly in finding candidates with sufficient, relevant experience, and secondly in convincing them and external observers that there is a genuine, important job for them to do, i.e. that this is not a token appointment.

Part of the problem is that there are few effective women's networks (and, indeed, those that exist may be counterproductive because they divert women's attention from real centres of power and influence). It is legitimate to seek out female independent directors in areas outside the business context (e.g. in government, civil service, the environment, voluntary sector work)—but not because they are the wives of influential people!

Those women's networks that do exist are sometimes less than helpful, too. For example, the annual Woman of the Year luncheon refused assistance to steer candidates towards independent director positions. The reason given: the event could not be allowed to have a commercial dimension! Yet many of these talented and energetic women would have been able to make a significant contribution to other boards.

It is also an impediment that some high-profile independent women directors do not give sufficient encouragement to other women with genuine potential. Even among those who do, it is not uncommon for prominent people to focus more on terminology (such as whether it is appropriate to refer to independent women directors as 'ladies') rather than the practicalities of creating openings.

Another frequent issue is time pressure. Even though our society may be becoming more egalitarian, women executives are rarely able to avoid some domestic responsibilities. As Rosemary Day, a director of Allied Dunbar and independent director of London Buses comments, 'You need to be very disciplined to be a female non-executive director. You have to plan at least six months ahead and be prepared to sacrifice your domestic life!'

To make up for a temporary shortage in director-level talent

Many companies are so busy developing good managers that they neglect to grow suitable board candidates. Appointing independent directors with the relevant background can provide a breathing space while internal candidates are put through fast-track development programmes that will equip them to play the director role. Typically, this would take about three years.

Many of the newly privatized companies in the 1980s brought independent directors on to the board for just this reason. Often lacking in commercial expertise (some, such as Royal Ordnance, did not even have sales and marketing departments), in profit management and in shareholder relations skills, it made sense to import those capabilities. The alternative would have been to replace whole layers of senior management with people from the private sector, with the result that much of the valuable technical and industry-specific expertise would have been lost.

Small companies, in particular, often have the additional difficulty that key managers often become so important in the structure that they expect rewards such as share options and directorships long before they are ready for them. Using executive directorships to buy their loyalty is a very short-sighted solution. A better solution is to appoint an independent director who can mentor the potential director, helping him or her to develop the skills and thinking patterns required. (This kind of mentoring relationship can continue after a board appointment, of course.)

To provide flexibility at the top

Different market conditions often require a different mix of skills and characteristics at board level. Changing the composition of the executive team can lead to disruption and panic in the organization. Changes among the independent directors may be barely noticed.

All of these are valid reasons for acquiring independent directors. Some less valid (but still common) reasons are detailed below.

To boost the status of the company

Having a few titles on the notepaper may make a company seem more respectable and solid, but the advantage is likely to be only temporary. Real reputations come from the way the company does business.

To gain access to the independent director's networks

Although in theory the independent director should be able to introduce the company to new business, in practice it usually does not work out that way. Many independent directors do not want to risk compromising their networks through overt selling. Moreover, while the network may accept the independent director in one role, it may not do so in another. A salutary case in point is a young public relations consultancy, which took on several independent directors largely because of their excellent contacts. One director, for example, had been head of a major employers' organization. This director used his network to make dozens of appointments with senior industry figures, who were of course polite enough to see him and the chief executive of the PR company. But polite chats are not the stuff of which business deals are made, especially when they are at too high a level. The independent director used up a lot of favours for no appreciable gain either to himself or the young business.

Municipal Mutual Insurance (MMI) undoubtedly had Maurice Stonefrost's public sector experience and networks in mind when it appointed him as an independent director in the late 1980s. MMI, which specialized in providing cover for local authorities, was able to draw on Stonefrost's background working at senior level for a variety of district and county councils including director general of the Greater London Council, and as chief executive of British Rail's pension fund. Not only could he make useful introductions, but he was also able to provide insights into how customers thought.

Promoting Stonefrost to non-executive chairman in 1990 may not have been such a wise move. By this time, the company had already sown the seeds of disaster and an experienced company doctor might in retrospect have been a more appropriate appointment.

Specific contributions of the independent director to the small company

The benefits already described apply, in various circumstances, to a wide range of companies. However, for the small company, there are some specific additional useful contributions an independent director can make. In addition to providing general business advice, he or she can help in reviewing issues such as

- Pricing policy
- Management information systems
- Credit control
- Compliance (e.g. with VAT, PAYE, National Insurance and Health and Safety requirements)
- Key appointments
- Personnel policies (especially recruitment and performance assessment)
- Pay and pensions
- Forcing through cultural change
- Maintaining and increasing quality consciousness
- Helping to draft and monitor social responsibility policies (e.g. equal opportunities)

The independent director can also, as several correspondents have commented to us, encourage executive directors and senior managers to have a go, to make mistakes and learn from them. Too often we reward long service rather than intelligent risk-taking.

When Nicholas Wills, then chairman of conglomerate BET, and Stephen Hayklan were put on to the advisory board of EDS (the electronic data subsidiary of General Motors) it was as much for their network as for their business acumen. The former offered a wide portfolio based on a lifetime in a diverse service group; the latter contributed special interests in former Eastern Europe and in Russia. However, neither was, nor should have been, appointed solely for his network. We have argued this point before in the book and will do so again. It is a difficult balance to strike, but if done sensitively the facility to produce a network *can* have its role in the criteria for appointing an independent director.

In one small publishing company, the key role of the independent director was to help the founders plan how to make the company saleable in three years' time. He helped the executives decide on potential acquirers to target and how to maximize the value of the company, as far as they were concerned. Inevitably, that meant taking a close look at management information systems and key personnel. The independent director did not get involved at a detailed level, he just kept asking questions at the board meeting until the necessary changes were made.

The other side of the coin is that companies can also benefit from encouraging their own executives to become independent directors, either on subsidiary boards, or on the board of a smaller customer or supplier. This is a relatively low cost method of assessing his or her ability, with the only downside being the loss of the young Turk's time when he or she is attending to his or her independent director responsibilities. Problems of confidentiality do not seem to be significant (anyone at this level should be fully capable of handling any that do arise anyway). Even if, as occasionally happens, the independent director leaves his or her main job to work full-time within the other company, this can be seen as a positive result—the precipitation of the inevitable in someone who should arguably not have been part of the succession plan anyway.

Where this approach works, the company also benefits from closer relationships with the partner organization.

Some companies have long recognized the value non-executive directorships add to the development of high-flyers. For example, ICI welcomes the opportunity for its board directors—including main board hopefuls serving on subsidiary boards—to take positions as non-executive directors with other companies. The rationale is that exposure to new business situations and alternative corporate cultures expands the horizons of top managers enabling them to make a greater contribution to the home board.

There are signs too that other companies are moving in the

same direction. It is a trend which augurs well both in terms of improving the calibre of non-executive directors serving on the boards of British companies and for personal development opportunities.

The calibre of British directors in the future will benefit greatly, the authors believe, from opportunities for managers to become independent directors at an earlier stage in their careers.

In the future, too, greater emphasis on matching the needs of individuals and the companies they work for with the non-executive director needs of host companies, is likely to improve the management talent base in Britain. For example, the *Annex Scheme*—devised by one of the authors and operated by headhunters Hanson Green—gives high-flyers with main board potential an opportunity to become non-executive directors on major subsidiary boards of other companies (see Figure 7.1).

It is a far cry from the traditional view of non-executive directors as the great and the good lending their names to a company's letterhead, or of so-called 'golfing partners' whose main qualification for the job was that of being a friend of the chairman.

Nor are non-executive director positions seen any longer as retirement presents. By the time an individual retires, many companies would argue, it is—or should be—too late. Those with the most valuable contribution to make are people at the peak of their careers, in their forties and early fifties. In most cases, too, they are also the ones with the most to gain.

According to Colin St Johnston, managing director of Promotion of Non-Executive Directors (PRO NED): 'Anybody who is a non-executive director needs to be actively involved in the commercial world. It is not appropriate for someone retired with no other business involvements'.

He could have added, in the end, real effectiveness depends more on style than factual contributions, on how the NED probes and contributes rather than on the contribution itself.

SUMMARY

Independent directors have developed almost by accident, so it is perhaps not surprising that confusion exists as to who makes a good independent director, what exactly should be expected of him or her, and what the job entails. Educating both companies and independent directors in how to maximize the contribution from this form of corporate governance is an urgent requirement.

REFERENCES

1. *The Board and the Non-Executive Director: Improving Boardroom Performance.* The PA Consulting Group, 1991.
2. Making the most of Non-Executive Directors—a survey by Hanson Green and The ITEM Group plc, 1992.
3. The Institutional Shareholders' Committee (ISC) code of best practice, 1991.
4. *Plc UK: A Focus on Corporate Trends.* 3i, 1992.
5. *Research into the Role of the Non-Executive Director.* PRO NED and the London Stock Exchange. PRO NED, 1992.
6. The Cadbury Committee Report on the Financial Aspects of Corporate Governance. May 1992.
7. Board of Directors Study, UK. Korn/Ferry International, 1992.
8. Charles Batchelor, Value for money from an outsider's view. *The Financial Times,* 20 March 1990.
9. Tom Nash, The growing power of non-executive directors. *The Director,* September 1989.
10. Maxwell beat watchdogs. *The Daily Telegraph,* 19 February 1992.
11. Jay Lorsch and Elizabeth McIver, *Pawns or Potentates: The Reality of America's Corporate Boards, The Financial Times.* McGraw-Hill and Harvard Business School, 1989.

2 Who are these independent directors and what do they do?

An independent director is (or should be) an independent voice appointed to the board to ensure that it does not become too internally focused. The actual role varies widely. Among the most common roles are:

- *Part-time chairman.*
- *Confidant(e) to the chief executive*—for example, the Japanese chief executive of a UK subsidiary of a large Japanese company appointed a senior British academic to help him acclimatize to British management thinking.
- *An expert with specialist knowledge not currently held within the executive ranks*—perhaps a manager with a strong understanding of the Brussels bureaucracy, or maybe even a headteacher whose knowledge of community issues may be valuable.
- *A community conscience*—for example, a chemicals company might appoint a prominent environmentalist.
- *A contact maker*—for example, someone who knows the market well at top management level. Defence firms often hire retiring senior civil servants from the Ministry of Defence as independent directors for a period while their contacts are still valuable.
- *Conferrer of status* (a company's respectability may be measured in many cases by the number of titles on its board). A name respected by City institutions is a common current qualification.

In addition, the independent director is likely to be part of key board committees, such as audit and executive remuneration, where, in theory at least, he or she can exercise restraint to balance the conflicting interests of the management and the shareholders.

Except for the first and last, all of these roles can potentially be performed in other ways. The CEO's confidant(e) may alternatively be a senior management consultant; the community conscience can be appointed to a policy advisory committee at a functional level in the organization, as IBM does in the majority of its operations outside the United States; contact makers can be tied in with agency agreements. The critical question is: *to what extent can the individual add greater value to the organization by being on the board than via some other kind of arrangement?* If the answer is none or very little, a board appointment would be viable if it is the only way to attract an exceptional individual, whom the company cannot afford to let pass. Even so, that individual must be capable of making a genuine contribution to boardroom discussions.

In the case of the CEO's confidant(e), there is an additional argument for not following the independent director route. To remain independent, it is important that an independent director should not become too close to the CEO; and even more importantly, should not be seen to do so. Patronage and independence do not fit well together. It can be argued, however, that a confidant(e) can advise the CEO best if he or she is present at the board meetings, because that is where key decisions are made. Compromise solutions include making the confidant(e) a non-voting member of the board; or making him or her only one of a number of independent directors. A small note of caution: some board meetings, even main board ones, often discuss a great deal of routine, mundane matters but then one person's mundane matter is another person's fresh challenge. However, the point does illustrate that the independent director's experience on a subsidiary board can be little more than routine. There is, often—usually—a world of difference between main and subsidiary board deliberations.

In his book, *Making it Happen*,[1] Sir John Harvey-Jones suggests five key roles, which he describes as:

- 'The Emperor's Clothes': having the confidence to ask naïve questions.

- 'The Oil Can': lubricating relationships.
- 'Bank of England': bringing famous name respectability.
- 'Father confessor': the wise confidant.
- 'High sheriff': riding into town to get rid of the chairman or other directors.

The actual roles an individual independent director takes will depend on a variety of factors, among them are the following:

- Background and experience.
- The situation of the company (start-up or mature, prospering or in trouble).
- The current composition of the board (a single independent director on a strong board may have very little influence; so might one independent director among a large group).
- Whether the chairman and CEO roles are split or combined (if they are combined, independent directors need to be especially strong and experienced to counterbalance any excesses by top management).
- The character of the chairman (is this someone of high moral integrity or a wheeler-dealer, for example?) A good personal 'fit' with the chairman is an essential prerequisite for a successful relationship.
- The manner of recruitment.

Of these, the latter is worth particular mention. When Professor Sir Roland Smith lost the chairmanship of British Aerospace, *The Times* reported:[2] 'One sage says: "He made the mistake of not appointing his own independent directors."' Perhaps, from a political survival point of view, it might have been to Smith's advantage. But packing the board with the chairman's cronies not only stifles dissent; it shuts off genuine discussion and argument as well. Independent directors appointed in such circumstances have little power or influence, because their role is seen to be to say yes.

The true colours of such independent directors often emerge when the company is in trouble or when there is a need to rock the boat on behalf of the shareholders. The wrong candidate in such circumstances will be tested and found wanting, because he or she will not be prepared to face adverse publicity. Or worse still, when such a person sees a problem which others either have not seen or do not wish to face, the same inappropriate candidate will pretend that the problem simply is not there and for the same personal reasons. The price paid when a firm appoints the wrong candidate can be very high.

The influence of the independent director can be substantial if he or she is chosen as the result of lengthy discussion by the board and detailed search to find the right candidate. At the other extreme, the independent director appointed because of social or personal connections (often referred to as 'golfing partners') with the chairman, may have no other credentials with the rest of the board. To be effective, an independent director must be seen by the majority of board colleagues to bring a valuable contribution in his or her own right. Status often depends on the method of selection or appointment.

In a survey we conducted recently[3] among independent directors (of which more later) the majority found that the manner of their appointment added to their status, or made no difference. This is not always the case, however. We have encountered cases where the bitter pill of enforced early retirement from an executive post has been sweetened with the offer of a non-executive role, for example.

For the rest of what independent directors do, we can simply say that they attend board meetings at regular intervals (usually every two or three months but in some cases monthly or even fortnightly) throughout the year. They may also be expected to attend some board subcommittees and major company events, such as Arts sponsorships. This is the minimum that might normally be expected, and although there are undoubtedly independent directors who simply read the papers for board meetings in the taxi on the way there, a conscientious independent director will become much more involved in the organization, trying to understand it sufficiently to make useful observations and suggestions, but not so closely that he or she is in danger of being absorbed within the mind-set of the executive team.

The independent director may also supplement what the

full-time executives do. There is a limit to what any full-time executive can handle. It might appear that a strong, determined chairman can inspire, cut, reorganize, and turn a company around single handedly, without the need of an independent director. But an independent director can help and should question a strong chairman to ensure that there is no halo effect determining the chairman's decisions.

And the impact? A study by *The Director* magazine in 1991[4] found no correlation between quoted company performance and whether a company had independent directors. Yet anecdotal evidence suggests strongly that independent directors have an important effect in helping to steer companies—especially small and medium sized enterprises—away from difficulties and in focusing the efforts of the executive team.

The conclusion we have been drawn to time and again is that there is not a paradox here. Where the right independent director is chosen, at the right time, the benefits can be out of all proportion to the minor costs of their services. The problem is that probably less than one in three appointments is made with the degree of care, understanding and commitment to fulfil the potential. For a great many companies, particularly quoted companies, independent directors will remain largely an irrelevance in terms of practical, positive impact on the company's fortunes, until the executive team takes the role seriously enough to expend the same energies in recruitment as they would on one of their own number.

WHAT SHOULD AN EFFECTIVE INDEPENDENT DIRECTOR DO?

Having identified a variety of roles that an independent director could be expected to play, it is now necessary to add some flesh to the bones. For while the effective independent director might meet all of these over a period of years, the ineffective independent director might meet none of them.

Here, we aim to explore in more detail what an independent director actually does (or should do), starting with the mundane and working up to the unusual. In doing so, we shall explore some of the skills an effective independent director needs.

For most independent directors, the time spent divides fairly easily into board meetings and 'the rest'. How they spend that time depends upon the consensus that the board reaches on what is expected of them. In many cases, the board meeting is the sole arena, in which the executive and non-executive directors meet, other than at sponsored social events. These independent directors, we believe, are inevitably handicapped when it comes to contributing significant insights into strategic issues—a superficial knowledge of personalities and issues does not encourage sensitive generation and evaluation of options.

At the other extreme, there are independent directors who find they spend a high proportion of their working week within the organization, responding to requests from executives and other managers. (It is very easy for this to happen, for example, within Training and Education Councils (TECs) or Hospital Trusts.) For these independent directors the danger is that the independence of view that represents their most valuable contribution at board level may be compromised by becoming too familiar with the organization. Once independent directors start to become part of the culture, once they cease to be surprised by things encountered, once they are able to second guess what most executives will say or do, it is probably time to reconsider whether a non-executive role is still practical in the circumstances. The dividing line between part-time executive and non-executive can be very thin.

John Moccata, a company doctor with a wide experience of company boards, offers the following useful generic job specification of the non-executive role:

- To ensure that the company produces timely and meaningful financial information to enable the board as a whole, and the non-executive director in particular, to monitor the company's progress and to identify problem areas and potential areas of growth as they arise.
- To advise the board on all areas of strategic planning with

particular reference to property investment, fund raising, corporate finance and mergers and acquisitions.

- To act as a sounding board for the executive directors on all management matters where an independent but critical viewpoint can be beneficial.
- To advise the board on the probable legal implications of potential or actual problems and proposed courses of action and suggest possible solutions.
- To advise the board on personnel issues such as the emoluments of directors and senior executives, share option schemes, pension schemes, etc.
- To undertake specific projects for the board in connection with any of the above matters.
- To be available for *ad hoc* discussions with executive directors on problems as they arise.
- To chair board meetings or meetings of subcommittees if so required.

WHO ARE THESE INDEPENDENT DIRECTORS?

The PA Consulting survey[5] showed a heavy imbalance in the composition of non-executives towards the Great and the Good. The typical independent director of a quoted company is chairman of at least one other quoted company.

According to the study by *The Director* magazine, he or she is likely to have an honour (most commonly CBE). Titles abound, with the most common being 'Sir, followed by Hon., Dr, Lord, Rt Hon. and Prof.'. The most common professional qualification, by five times, is the accountant's FCA.

The heavy imbalance of the Great and the Good is quite frankly a deplorable situation, not least because it denies the opportunity of really useful people to contribute, to the benefit of shareholders and other directors.

There are some active independent directors, who do nothing else. Often retired, they have a portfolio of non-executive directorships that keeps them happily employed. There are reportedly a handful of individuals who have collected several dozen independent director positions and juggle them continuously. The problem here is that they lack the anchor of a current executive position. It is very easy for them to slip into the role of business dilettante, never having enough involvement in any company to take responsibility for seeing things through. They also tend to get out of touch very quickly.

Some successful chairmen, often strong and arrogant, sometimes recommend independent director appointments on to other boards or merely as a method of paying back former favours. These appointees are usually of a similar position and have equal status and sometimes even of a similar age. They either do not take the appointment seriously or they do not understand the nature of the independent director appointments.

At the other extreme, if these professional independent directors are conscientious, they may easily find themselves sucked into spending near full-time in a particularly demanding company. Whereas typical independent directors know that their prime responsibility is to their executive job and so find it relatively easy to limit involvement to policy and strategy issues, professional independent directors have only the restraints of their other commitments (and physical exhaustion). This full-time part-time status can be extremely frustrating, for while independent directors share all the problems of their executive colleagues, they are unlikely to have the same level of information or infrastructural support.

The percentage of board seats taken by non-executive directors rose from 33 per cent in 1985 to 44 per cent in 1991. A number of factors suggest that the pool from which those positions are filled will have to be expanded in the next few years.

Recent scandals, such as the Mirror Group pension fraud, will add to public pressure for more effective corporate policing. At the same time, the Cadbury Committee—set up to investigate the whole issue of corporate governance—gave an added spur to the recruitment of new independent directors by rejecting the idea that individuals should hold multiple non-executive directorships.

For their part, host companies value non-executive directors because they bring an outsider's view to the board. Effective independent directors make an important contribution as lateral thinkers and specialists, as well as in the corporate police officer role.

Most independent directors are appointed by the chairman, or the board. Occasional attempts by individual shareholders to have themselves elected as independent directors tend to be distinguished by their lack of success. Veteran campaigner Noel Falconer, for example, has been frustrated by institutional shareholders in his ambitions to become independent director of British Gas, British Telecom and North West Water. The problem is simply that it normally requires a demonstration of blatant incompetence or maladministration before institutional shareholders—who usually hold the bulk of the shares—will vote against the incumbent management team. Falconer is campaigning for changes in the legislation that would reduce the voting power of institutions *vis-à-vis* the individual shareholder.

Occasionally, independent directors are appointed by the banks, usually when a company is in crisis, unable to repay its debts. Because they are normally reluctant to appoint any but the most senior and experienced people as independent directors, and because these people are in short supply, the banks frequently make the appointment too late for effective turnaround. The painful decline of Dunlop Holdings a decade ago remains a classic example of this process at work. The banks only made their own appointments when there was insufficient cash to maintain the business. Executive management then all but disappeared, as even minor expenditure with guaranteed return was held up by the independent director-dominated board. Instead of bleeding to death, Dunlop was eventually strangled by its bankers. Yet it could have been saved with earlier, more diligent attention.

The banks and the companies concerned would both be better served if lesser-known independent directors were appointed when major loans were first granted. These individuals could then act as eyes and ears, providing timely warning of difficulties ahead and perhaps changing the executive management before the crisis strikes.

Some independent directors gain their position as a phased retirement from executive directorship. A strong executive chairman or chief executive may remain on the board as an independent director to help a successor settle in (or, less positively, to make sure the successor does not do anything the independent director would not do). Some companies use independent director positions to put displaced executives out to grass gently, with minimum loss of face. Worst of all is the situation where a long-serving and trusted employee is given an independent director post as a retirement present, along with the gold clock. If the objective is to give the employee a reason to get up in the morning, to help the employee stave off digging into his or her capital, or simply to keep out from under the spouse's feet, then there are much better solutions.

This is not to say that retired executives are automatically inappropriate. The key factors are motivation, competence and currency of knowledge and networks. Dr Brian Smith, for example, explains his motivation as follows:

> Someone like me who has retired from executive roles because they don't want all the work that goes with it can be pulled in for an independent director position. I retired two years ago and said I would not take another CEO position, but I'm here for advice to support a first class chief executive like John Egan at BAA. It's the elder statesman role, but it has to be someone with enough gunsmoke in his nose to still know what it's all about.

However, Smith is adamant that a retiree's value to the board runs out. He maintains:

> Appointments should be for three years, with possibly a second term and then that's it, a bit like American presidents. If someone has retired that takes them up to six years past retirement and by then it is time to go. By having the system formalised you can avoid bruised egos.
>
> Also, it ensures a constant supply of new blood coming onto the board and saying 'why do you do it like that?', which is very important because you often find you don't have an answer!

Most independent directors are from a business background, but a small proportion come from areas such as education, the Armed Services and Diplomatic Services. The contribution they bring is somewhat different and needs to be even more tightly defined than for an independent director from business. The specialist logistics skills of the senior army officer, for example, can be extremely valuable in a distribution business; similarly, the negotiating skills of the experienced diplomat can be ideally suited to developing trade links in new territories.

THE IDEAL INDEPENDENT DIRECTOR

- *is aged 38 to 55.* Below the mid-thirties, he or she is unlikely to have had the breadth and depth of experience to make a pragmatic contribution. Very few people acquire sufficient *gravitas* to be taken seriously in the role before that age. Over 60 and he or she may not have the drive or energy to see major changes through. Moreover, if the candidate is about to retire, then the currency of contacts, knowledge and following of business trends will diminish rapidly. Within two years of retirement, 50 per cent of most people's contacts will have become obsolete. At the same time, for a retired person, the independent director salary may begin to assume too much importance to be able to put it at risk by disagreeing with the executive line. An independent director cannot be independent unless he or she knows it is possible to quit tomorrow without feeling the financial loss.

  Of course, there are also some excellent independent directors well into their sixties, seventies and even eighties. Still young in heart and mind, well able to remember previous business cycles, they can provide a strong stabilizing influence. However, such independent directors are relatively rare.
- *has learnt the hard way the importance of cash flow and strong earnings per share*—and will always bring discussions back to these considerations.
- *is more than busy enough already.* Any executive who has not too much to do cannot be looking hard enough. The fact is, effective executives always make time for important activities. If they see an independent director post as important to their own development or interests, they will make the time to do the job properly. The *ineffective*

executive, however, is likely to make an ineffective independent director. They can be seen typically turning up to meetings with the papers unread, often having to leave for another appointment half-way through.

- *has the courage to stand up and be counted*—yet is sufficient of a team player to work harmoniously with the rest of the board. Says Sara Morrison, an executive director of Abbey National, GEC and independent director of Rover Learning Business: 'On an effective board, the directors have sufficient regard and respect for each other to have blinding rows. It mustn't be polite and cosy; rather it should cover all sorts of contentious issues. Even when we are cursing and blinding, we all know we are on the same side. We may be argumentative, but we know the rules and are frank.'

  The independent director who lacks the courage to force issues when it matters is in reality a negative influence on the company—for he or she lulls the executive into thinking that alternative views really have been considered, when they have not.

- *is able to express ideas clearly and concisely.* Often, the greatest benefit an independent director brings is the discipline and clarity of thought otherwise lacking in an executive team, where all the old arguments have been rehearsed to death.

- *has the presence to take over as chairman, if required.* The issue of whether to combine or separate the roles of chairman and CEO generates heated debate, but our experience suggests strongly that the chairman should be non-executive or part-time executive, so that he or she has a healthy connection to the outside world.

In short, the ideal independent director has many of the same characteristics as a key executive director—and should be selected with the same degree of care and deliberation. The right independent director for a particular company may be known to the CEO already, through the golf club or the local branch of the CBI; but it is an arrogant chairman indeed who assumes the best candidates will automatically be numbered among acquaintances.

Equally, such paragons of virtue are not abundant, at least, not from traditional sources. Stephen Walls, until recently chief executive of Arjo Wiggins Appleton, knew precisely the kind of independent director candidate he needed to help him take his company to the Stock Market. Although he sought several, however, he only found one—the finance director of a retail bank, who had previous experience in the paper industry. Walls told *The Independent*:[6]

> I could have filled the slots ten times over if all I had wanted was a name and someone who turned up to lunch occasionally. It is more difficult to find people at the peak of their careers who can afford to spend the necessary amount of time on the company. It is especially difficult if you are looking for people from overseas to reflect the global nature of the business.

SPECIAL SITUATIONS

The non-executive chairman

The argument over whether the chairman should be executive or non-executive, and whether the two roles should or should not be combined in one individual, has never been satisfactorily resolved.

Clare Hogg writing in *The Times*,[7] puts the case for separating the roles:

> The pace of change in business now is such that unless much thought is given to strategy and direction, a company cannot hope to survive and, in general, the managing director is too bogged down in detail or corporate energizing to have the serenity and perspective to do this.

She points out too that the board itself needs managing and that this is a job better carried out by a non-executive member:

> If, as the Institute of Directors defines it, the board is the Mind and Will of the company, it is critical that that Mind and that Will are properly orchestrated to produce a melodious tune.

It seems that this is one of the few areas in which Britain is ahead of the United States. Harvard professor, Jay Lorsch, carried out some research which revealed that only 17 per cent of American companies had a separate chairman and CEO. He confirms that the argument that it is not easy to define what the chairman will do if he or she is not the CEO and is not to be a strawman is a compelling one for many CEOs. 'What underlies all these objections is that CEOs are afraid of losing their power and of their jobs becoming complicated,' he says. 'Some whom I talked with are really most concerned that their predecessor might be appointed as their chairman. They're making all kinds of excuses because they find it hard to be objective.' An American analogy is given by a chairman quoted in the *The Corporate board*: 'When he got into trouble, President Nixon was both the head of state and head of government, so both were in trouble. Therefore, there was no opportunity to carry on "above the fray".'

Over double the number of companies have full-time chairmen as opposed to part-time chairmen. This is not necessarily such a good arrangement. Denis Cassidy, chairman of three retail public limited companies comments: 'It is a valid criticism that if you have both a chairman and chief executive working full-time they might fall over each other eventually. So you ensure that the chairman has a degree of part-timeness, depending on the stages of the business cycle.'

According to Clare Hogg, where the traditional company chairman may have had a staid and conservative image, now he or she needs to be 'a racier individual altogether'. Peter Gummer, the chairman of Shandwick, gives an excellent description of what it feels like to be a chairman today in *A Head for Business:*

> My job is like driving a motor car, preferably quite a fast motor car. If you concern yourself with what is happening just over the edge of the bonnet when you are driving a Ferrari Testarossa, you will drive into a lamp post ... the faster you're driving the further down the road you look. You must be conscious of the turning to the left or right, but there are other people around to study the side roads.

The combined chairman and chief executive role is generally

not a good idea for large companies, but as Hogg points out, there are situations where it does make sense.

> The size of the company is an important consideration ... Anthony Fuller, chairman of Fuller, Smith and Turner, is a good example. For more than a decade he succeeded in combining both roles. As he explains, 'the company was small enough to make a combined chairman-managing director role perfectly viable'. When he vacated the managing director slot he continued as chairman.

In larger companies, and there are still a fair number in the United Kingdom where the executive chairman remains unchallenged by a separate chief executive, there is a particular need for heavy representation of independent non-executive directors, according to the Institutional Shareholders' Committee. Big institutions may want to pack company boards with part-time independent directors, but they find it hard to find people of the right calibre to represent shareholders (although PRO NED and non-executive director search specialists Hanson Green report no shortage). They are reluctant to suggest structural solutions such as two-tier boards (as they have in some continental countries), or legal recognition of non-executive directors as a separate category for fear that other interest groups, trade unions for example, may also demand representation. Non-executives working solely as representatives of shareholders who may come and go is not the answer either.

However, while there is a long list of corporate disasters among companies led by combined chairman/CEOs, there is also evidence from accountants Arthur Andersen[8] that these managers tend to be more conservative.

Where the independent director takes on the chairman's role, it must be recognized that a much greater level of commitment to the company is needed.

At its simplest, the role of a chairman has four main parts:

- To lead the board meetings.
- To represent the company to the outside world—in particular, shareholders, to the City and the Stock Exchange, and to peers.

- To set the moral tone and vision for the company.
- To weld the executives and independent directors into a team.

Leading the board meeting

The independent chairman brings an element of balance to the board. The chief executive is in effect the leader of the executive team. An executive chairman inevitably absorbs some of this role, taking away some of the authority and influence of the chief executive. The more he or she does so, the more difficult it is to act as leader of the whole team of directors. If the roles of chairman and chief executives are combined, it becomes even more difficult. The independent chairman has the advantage of only having to exert leadership at the board meetings.

Representing the company to the outside world

One of the problems for an executive chairman is that he or she is frequently put in the position of *defending* top management and its strategy. The independent chairman has the advantage of being sufficiently removed from day-to-day management to be seen as a relatively impartial observer. Indeed he or she may be seen by shareholders as more on 'their' side than on that of the executives.

On the other hand, the lower level of involvement of the independent chairman in strategic planning and implementation may make him or her less credible to a City audience. Stockbrokers' analysts and fund managers, for example, tend to value hearing about a company and its plans from the person responsible for making it happen—the CEO. Many companies find that the combination of a strong CEO and an influential independent chairman captures the best of both worlds.

Setting the moral tone and vision

The independent chairman, having a visible existence outside the company, is better able to represent the moral tone and its social values of the company.

Welding the executives and independent directors into a team

There is a world of difference between preventing conflict among the members of the board and creating a well-integrated team of directors committed to the same long-term objectives. The chairman has to maintain a balance between allowing the independent directors to become too closely identified with the executives (losing their critical edge) and allowing them to hinder executives in getting on with growing and managing the company. By the same token, a 'policing' role for independent directors—as recommended by some observers—would undermine the chairman's attempt to forge a coherent team.

It requires a deft hand to steer between these conflicting demands. But the capable chairman will extract the best from both the executives and the independent directors, stimulating the one to develop and implement viable strategies, and the other to provide constructive challenge and relevant guidance.

The benefits of an independent chairman

An independent chairman:

- makes it easier to split the roles of chairman and chief executive—it largely avoids the potential clash between two strong characters at the top, where, for all practical purposes, there is usually only room for one. Although executive chairmen are still in the majority, we expect the pendulum increasingly to swing in favour of non-executives in the 1990s.
- has a broader view of the industry, not having come up

through the ranks of that organization, and, in many cases, coming from outside the sector entirely.

- is less likely to become involved in company politics.
- can be appointed more readily and more rapidly than an executive chairman—allowing a more rapid response to the company's circumstances. In particular, as a company doctor, the independent chairman can initiate a prompt rescue approach, as for example, at jewellers Ratners.
- can be extremely helpful if the company is contemplating a float, especially if well connected in the City and has been through flotations before (a lot of unnecessary executive director time and money can otherwise be wasted learning the ropes).
- is especially valuable for the family firm, where a strong hand at the top is often lacking and introversion is often a fact of life. An independent chairman can act as mediator between family interests, and balance long- and short-term goals. According to Sir James Ackers, former chairman of West Midlands Health Authority and former chairman of the British Chamber of Commerce, three-quarters of family firms in the Midlands lack the appropriate type of chairman.

In general, an independent chairman is less powerful than an executive chairman, if only because he or she is not around as much. However, if the independent chairman has been brought in for a specific purpose, with a strong mandate from shareholders and other investors, he or she may in fact be *more* powerful.

The role of independent deputy chairman is less well documented, but also becoming increasingly common. Effectiveness in this role depends in large part upon being able to take a back seat, yet being prepared to step into the lead when required. The authors hope to carry out further research into this role, which appears in many cases to have quite a few similarities with that of Vice-President of the United States—largely ceremonial, but with awesome potential.

Not surprisingly, independent chairmen have their own strong views. For example, Dr Brian Smith, independent chairman of BAA and independent director of Cable and Wireless and Berisford:

> I don't actually believe there is such a thing as a non-executive chairman, but there are part-time chairmen as I am here [BAA]. A chairman has different sorts of responsibilities to the other independent directors. My job as chairman is to manage the board. The CEO's job is to manage the company. As chairman I make sure issues come out clearly and fairly. That means ensuring the board's processes are fair and open.
>
> I always say that at BAA John Egan does all the work. He thinks so too. That's how it should be if you're doing the job properly. My job as chairman is to keep things ticking at the top. If the chairman and CEO try to do each other's jobs they can easily divide the organization because people will play them off against each other.

The independent chairman and the chief executive

Of all boardroom relationships, this is the one that *must* work if the company is to have clear, effective direction. When the relationship is based on mutual respect and understanding and on clear demarcation of roles, it allows both parties, even if they are equally strong-willed, the room to operate as they believe is right. The only significant opportunities for discussion or conflict are then major issues of policy, ethics or competence.

Dr Brian Smith describes how he and Sir John Egan (both strong, purposeful characters) divide the leadership role:

> John Egan is a great leader-stirrer and a great consumer man. He firmly believes that the consumer is king. He has changed BAA from a technically competent company to one that is also customer focused. John is very good at challenging people and throwing out demands. As CEO, that is his job. If he has a hobby-horse, you can be sure that he will ride it hard. He has a very different style to me, but I agree with his methods. The reason we work well together is that although we have different ways of working, we share the same values and the same philosophy towards business. That's very important if you are going to work well with someone. As a result, we complement each other—that's how the chairman and CEO roles work best.

Changing the management team

If the evidence of some of the more recent City scandals is anything to go by, independent directors are often reluctant to do anything about poor executive management until it is too late. Where the independent directors are in a majority and where executive managers have not deliberately concealed information, there really is little excuse for not taking appropriate action. After all, the warning signs of a company heading for difficulty are rarely isolated—they tend to come in clusters sufficient to raise doubts in even the myopic. In such cases, the board can and should require changes to occur and, if these are not forthcoming, should insist on its right to appoint a new chairman and/or chief executive.

Where the independent directors are in the minority, it becomes much more difficult. In practice, they have to obtain the backing of major shareholders to convene an extraordinary general meeting and push through the recommended changes. In many ways, the independent directors in this situation are like an opposition party in a parliament where the government has a large working majority. Unless there is evidence of severe malpractice or major losses leading to collapse of share prices, investors are by and large disinterested in intervening in corporate governance, preferring instead to show their disapproval by moving their investment elsewhere.

The executive team has most of the cards in its hands. It has access to all the advisers, consultants and information it needs to make its own case to institutions—and, most importantly, the money and time to put its case together. The situation is very similar to that of fund managers, who want to change the management in one of their investments. Alistair Blair, former corporate finance director of Fidelity Investments, drew on his own experience when he wrote in *The Financial Times*:[9]

> You need time because there is now going to be a serious fight. You are not just challenging management decisions, but the very livelihoods of the managers. The stakes for them are much higher than for you, and they will fight hard.

Of course, the task can be easier when the executive team is disunited, with an existing opposition group among the senior managers and individual directors. However, the independent director needs to take great care not to end up playing corporate politics for their own sake. In such situations, says David O'Shaugnessy, former executive director and now non-executive director of CarnaudMetalbox:

> In my experience these sorts of situations usually arise because executives seek a change at the helm. They then seek the assistance of the independent directors to bring about a change that they are unable to bring about themselves because of their own executive positions. It is much easier for the independent directors to ask the chairman to go, or to bring pressure to bear where it is needed to bring about the desired results.

The remarkable thing is how often independent directors do take the bull by the horns.

In April 1992, for example, non-executive directors at General Motors led by John Smale intervened to demote two of the company's top managers, including the right-hand man of Robert Stempel, the chairman. In what Martin Dickson described in *The Financial Times*[10] as, 'a remarkable display of muscle-flexing by non-executive directors', they also changed the functions of the board's executive committee—which theoretically wielded power between board meetings but in practice rarely met—to make it a more active force. At its head they installed Smale himself to ensure that Stempel's day-to-day running of the business would be accompanied by a more comprehensive flow of information to directors.

At Chrysler, too, independent directors showed their mettle by resisting efforts by Lee Iacocca to stay on as chairman after his retirement date. And, in 1991, the board of Compaq Computer dismissed Rod Canion, chief executive and co-founder of the business, in a disagreement over poor results and management style.

In Britain, the chairman of Barclays Bank, Sir John Quinton, was persuaded to give up his executive duties earlier than he had intended. Allied to concern about Barclay's slide in performance was Quinton's questionable decision to take on the time-consuming chairmanship of England's new Premier Soccer Division.

Robert Horton, the short-lived chairman and chief executive of British Petroleum, is a classic example. Under his leadership the board insisted on maintaining the dividend despite its being uncovered by earnings. 'Project 1990', an ambitious blueprint for change which encompassed such theories as empowerment, teamwork, delayering and so on was foisted on the company in a way which contradicted the very environment it was trying to introduce. On 25 June 1992 Horton was made to resign by the company's nine non-executive directors. Lord Ashburton, the non-executive director who led the coup took on the job of chairman.

Nick Kochan, author of *The Guinness Affair*,[11] writes in a recent study commissioned by the business school IMD, 'Saunders carried the can because for the public and the City, he was Mr Guinness. But Saunders was also chief executive of a board of directors who signally failed to exercise control over an all-powerful leader. This board has been almost completely thrown out.'

One problem identified by Kochan was the fact that many of the board were family members whose place on the board was inherited rather than earned. And as Jonathan Guinness frankly admitted they 'were not going to argue with someone who was making the shares worth more'. Out of 22 directors, the Guinness family accounted for nine. Saunders was brought in to turn the business around. His personal hidden agenda on joining Guinness in 1981 was to bypass the family shareholders and remove them. After a series of Machiavellian reorganizations, Saunders called the entire Guinness board at short notice. For some it was the first they had heard officially about their company's takeover of Distillers. Jonathan Guinness's reaction was 'Oh my God, how awful. This is terrible. Ernest has got megalomania.' Oliver Roux, the Guinness financial director comments: 'The non-executives could have said "no", but there was great pressure on them not to.' Right to the end, the directors who were members of the family were not convinced of Saunders's wrongdoing. Sir Norman Macfarlane was appointed chairman of a separate committee of non-executives included in the main board at the insistence of the Bank of England. This committee, once suspicious of malpractice, was forced to act independently right up to the board meeting where its members dramatically demanded that Saunders should step down.

The initiative to change the executive leadership may come from investors, from the independent directors themselves or from the executives—but it is the independent directors who make the decision. BAA's Dr Brian Smith puts the issues in perspective:

> If you can't resolve it then one of them has to go. The leadership role only works as long as people follow. If you have conflict, the leadership role will be the first casualty. The executive team don't usually gang up as such, but they should regard the independent directors as people they can talk to in confidence and air their concerns. Independent directors sitting in on board meetings can tell if something's not right. If the independent directors were worried they would have a meeting among themselves to discuss it. The essence of their role is that they are sufficiently independent to take any necessary action.
>
> Independent directors are in the position of saying either he goes or we go, which is a powerful lever because a chairman or CEO knows that if the independent directors resign together then the outside world knows there is a problem. But to walk away is a cop-out on your responsibilities as a director, so it is a last resort. As a director you're there to sort things out for the shareholders and the people who work for the company. The threat of resignation is itself very powerful.

According to Pat Rich of BOC, there are times too when a gentler approach is called for:

> In many situations Dutch Uncle skills are more useful than the hatchet-men style that some non-executive directors adopted in the past. Only a vote by the board can ultimately stop a strong-willed chief executive. Often, the best solution is to use the collective force of the non-executive directors at board meetings. You have to take the view, too, that if a chief executive doesn't kill the company, then he probably does know better than you.

Choosing a new chairman

While the need to select a new chairman may arise only occasionally, it will none the less be a particularly time-consuming task. The board as a whole will normally decide the characteristics it is looking for in the new appointment and shortlist the candidates. In most cases, the candidates will come from one of two sources: their own number, or an experienced individual from outside the company.

In making the decision, the board should consider a number of issues, well before it begins discussing actual candidates. Among, them:

- Should the position be executive or non-executive?
- What do we feel about combining the chairman/chief executive positions?
- What are the main issues the company is going to face over the next five years, and what sort of experience will a chairman need to lead us through the period?

The board should also review some of the generic skills and qualities an effective chairman demonstrates:

- The ability to manage senior level meetings in an organized, purposeful way.
- The self-awareness not to try to dominate proceedings.
- An openness with information between both executive and non-executive colleagues.
- The personal presence to be able to represent the board (and the company) to audiences—both internal and external.
- Credibility within the business sector.
- The ability to weld together both an executive team and a broader team consisting of all the board members.
- The ability to listen and keep his own counsel when needed.

Acquisitions, mergers and takeovers

Business as usual goes by the board for all executives when a major change in the composition or ownership of the company is in the air. If the company is the intended acquirer, the independent directors have a responsibility for tempering the executives' enthusiasm, for ensuring that the potential acquisition will bring the benefits expected and that the impact of the acquisition has been thought through properly. More medium to large companies fail from ill-judged acquisitions than from almost any other cause.

If the independent director takes this responsibility seriously, he or she must expect to spend a lot more time than normal, examining the information available, insisting that auditors obtain more information where there is any possibility of skeletons in the cupboard and establishing whether the acquisition is truly value for the shareholders' money. The independent director may well become unpopular with the executives—people do not like to be told that they cannot have the new toy they have set their sights on!

Hostile takeover bids demand even more input of time by the non-executives. The board as a whole must make up its collective mind as to whether the bid should be accepted or fought and, if the latter, what defensive strategies to adopt. All directors, both executive and independent, are likely to be drawn into the production of defence documents and lobbying of both the Press and the institutional investors. This is where some independent directors make their greatest (sometimes their only) significant contribution. They may be the only directors with this kind of experience, while the potential acquirer may have a whole team with relevant experience.

Such crises often increase team cohesion at the top, says Clive Bastin: 'It often pulls together any disagreements which might exist between executive and independent directors. In one case the atmosphere was considerably improved at the board level as a result of fighting off a hostile takeover bid.'

Of course, the independent directors may not necessarily agree with the executives on what is the best response to a hostile bid. Recalls Peter Sheldon, chairman of Stirling Group:

The UDS takeover battle was a classic example of independent directors versus executive directors. The executive directors wanted to recommend an offer of 130p per share from Bassie-shaw [Gerald Ronson's company], whilst two of the three independent directors felt that they were duty bound to recommend an offer of 132p from Hanson. The former felt that the interests of employees would be better protected under the Ronson offer and that the extra 2p did not justify accepting the Hanson offer. The independent directors [both 'City'] felt that price was all. A battle royal ensued with both camps setting out their views to shareholders. The independent directors won and Hanson gained control. I was on the losing side!

Rights issues

Most of the broad questions relating to a rights issue should have been covered at board meetings. However, the independent director has a responsibility to ensure that claims made in the issue documents are not misleading. He or she will probably need to spend time going over key points with some of the senior managers concerned—if only for self-protection. The independent director can also provide useful insights into how the investment community might react to particular statements, based on experience in his or her own company.

The owner-manager

The independent director on a board, where the majority of shares is owned by one or more of the executive team, is in a particularly difficult situation, not least because it is difficult to disentangle the various stakeholder interests and because all the power in the company is concentrated in one group.

In practice, effective independent directors in this situation tend to act as 'favoured friends'. Their role is part counsellor, part challenger and stimulator of new ideas. Frequently, they will meet with the owner-managers separately from the board, helping them to clarify their own objectives and how to mesh these with the company objectives. At board meetings, the independent directors can be helpful in encouraging those executives, who do not own substantial blocks of shares, to speak their mind and play a strong role. This may not be entirely acceptable to the owner-managers, if they are self-made entrepreneurs. The independent directors may then be forced into deciding whether they really can contribute to the company in the circumstances.

An anecdote from Robert Heller, former editor of *Management Today* and himself an independent director of a number of companies, points out the sorts of frustrations independent directors can be exposed to. In one case, says Heller, the chief executive and major shareholder decided to move to much more expensive premises without consulting the independent directors. The upshot of the move was to leave the company badly under-capitalized and vulnerable. Yet, he concedes, the independent directors were themselves partly to blame for encouraging him to think big and then failing to keep his feet on the ground.

Another problem, according to Heller, is that by the time small companies appoint independent directors it is often too late for them to be effective: the company is already under-capitalized, with independent directors in that situation powerless to do anything except make concerned noises at board meetings.

SUMMARY

Well chosen and well used, an independent director can be a remarkable asset to the company lucky enough to acquire him or her. In the smaller company, in particular, he or she can be the cause of a radical transformation or rejuvenation. Although, traditionally, independent directors have been drawn from a very narrow background, this is changing as boards demand more substantial, relevant contributions from non-executives. The ways in which companies *can* use independent directors are much broader than those in which they typically *do*.

In the following chapters, we will explore how to find and keep good independent directors and how to extract the best value from their services.

REFERENCES

1. Sir John Harvey-Jones, *Making it Happen: Reflections on Leadership.* Collins, 1988.
2. Judi Bevan, Corporate champion who defied the tanks. *The Times,* 3 February 1992.
3. Making the most of Non-Executive Directors—a survey by Hanson Green and The ITEM Group plc, 1992.
4. Tom Nash, Do these men deliver? *The Director,* October 1991.
5. *The Board and the Non-Executive Director: Improving Boardroom Performance.* The PA Consulting Group, 1991.
6. Clare Dobie, Rare species in Britain's boardrooms. *The Independent,* 2 February 1992.
7. Clare Hogg, The mind and the will. *The Times,* 25 June 1992.
8. *The Arthur Andersen Corporate Register.* Hemmington Scott Publishing Ltd, November 1991.
9. Alistair Blair, A coalition versus a dictator. *The Financial Times,* 27 May 1992.
10. Martin Dickson, Impatient GM board flexes its muscles. *The Financial Times,* 8 April 1992.
11. Nick Kochan, *The Guinness Affair.* Index, 1987.

3 Why do people become independent directors?

'When I actually think of the difficulties of being a good non-executive director, it amazes me that any of us bother at all,' says Sir John Harvey-Jones in his book *Making it Happen.*[1] 'It certainly cannot be for the money since in the United Kingdom non-executive directors are, in my view, extremely poorly rewarded if they do the job properly and perhaps over-rewarded if they are merely "there for the beer".'

Just as there are all sorts of independent directors, so there is a wide range of motivations. At the bottom end of the pile in value terms there are undoubtedly those independent directors, often local dignitaries on a pension, who do it mainly for the money. While they may be useful as contact makers, these independent directors are usually not really independent, because they cannot afford to give up the salary and therefore cannot afford to force the issue if they disagree with executive decisions. Indeed, a cardinal rule in appointing independent directors is never to consider anyone who needs the money.

Almost as serious, in terms of unsuitability, is the person who is motivated primarily by the status an independent director position brings. The effective independent director should have sufficient personal standing.

WHY DO TALENTED MANAGERS BECOME INDEPENDENT DIRECTORS?

Harvey-Jones[1] says that in a lot of cases it is seen as an opportunity for self-development. 'There is little doubt in my personal experience', he says, 'that the task of becoming a non-executive director of another company is the biggest learning experience of all for a professional businessman'.

Effective independent directors accept the position for a variety of more positive reasons, some of which are described below.

The challenge of a new business area

One of the lessons new independent directors often learn soonest is that there is no such thing as a unique business problem; that their experience in solving problems in the companies, where they are executives, is readily transferable. The confidence they acquire from this knowledge benefits their executive job as well, resulting in increased energy and ideas. They may often discover skills they did not know they had.

A frequent observation by independent directors is that spouses and friends find it hard to understand why they do it. The answer they most commonly give is that they *believe* in it as an important source of mutual benefit.

Terry Collins is non-executive chairman of Cranfield Conference Services, a small company started by Cranfield Institute of Technology in 1986, to provide conference facilities. He told *The Director* in 1989:[2] 'Although I am only involved in CCS from time to time, because it is a small business I feel I can really touch it. It's a great pleasure, especially when you have spent years in much larger companies where you tend to feel rather remote from the cutting edge of the business.'

Broadening their experience

Most British directors have little or no experience at a senior level outside their sector. Yet the requirement of the 1990s will increasingly be for executives with the breadth of experience to establish commercial alliances across sectors. An independent director post often also helps the incumbent to recognize what is special about his or her own company's management systems and practices. It is surprising how often other members of the host company board regard as original a comment which simply reflects normal practice in the independent director's own company.

As one observer comments: 'Companies believe it is a valuable experience for their executives to have a wider knowledge and exposure. Preferably it should be in different sectors to their own where, for instance, their functional knowledge makes them an asset to the company whose board they sit on.'

Says Sir Nigel Mobbs, chairman of Slough Estates: 'Generally speaking, directors who have no outside appointments tend to be rather introspective and protective and do not view problems objectively. Exposure to other people's problems can be valuable.'

Interest in helping smaller organizations grow

The managing director of one of the UK's largest insurance companies became an independent director of a small publishing company in large part to 'go back to the roots' of management—to become involved in a small venture with the potential to take off. He joined at the most exciting time, when the groundwork for expansion was being laid, and when he could have a valuable input, having experienced the problems of rapid growth in his own company. An interest in the business area and an existing friendship with some of the directors eased his involvement. As it happened, the independent director soon after quit his main job to join another start-up operation. He kept his independent director involvement, not least because it provided another forum in which to explore growth issues now of interest to both organizations.

However, the experienced independent director should also beware of allowing the smaller company to become reliant on him or her.

Developing their networks

Sitting on other people's boards opens new sets of doors. One of the most important benefits for an independent director is the opportunity the position provides for building up contacts and becoming better known. Joining a board is rather like joining a club or society. It opens up a whole new world, and it broadens the individual's horizons.

For example, John Burke, CEO of the chemical group Porton International and former main board director of Glaxo, joined the special advisory board for the Admiralty, which will determine the future structure of the Royal Navy. He learnt a great deal—and so did the Royal Navy.

Getting a feel for business trends

This can be invaluable for a senior manager. Good managers ensure they remain informed about new developments. Reading helps, so does subscribing to surveys or joining a trade association. But meeting people is the best method, particularly when it includes people outside one's immediate circle. The independent director automatically gains another circle of contacts while still remaining in the previous one.

Trevor Toolan, when main board director at British Rail, found his involvement in Young Enterprise, the initiative where business helps the young to learn about commercial life by actually running a company of their own creation, offered him excellent additional business antennae. Toolan was able to assess different business trends via those tutoring the young and over a period of time.

Indeed, some companies join and participate in a representative body, such as their own trade association, or with a more generalist one, such as the CBI and Institute of Directors, largely because they see in membership a facility to network. It is almost as if a member company joins the organization, regarding the membership and more specifically those chosen to get directly involved, as a sort of independent director role.

Learning from other companies, lessons they can apply in their own

The host company's mistakes—even if they have only just been experienced—can provide valuable clues to potential problems closer to home. For example, Jeffrey Jenkinson has learnt from his involvement in the public sector. As an executive director of the Port of London Authority (PLA) he has experienced the difficulties of non-executive directors being appointed by government under a statutory framework. Ports are commercial businesses and privatization is bringing a more flexible approach to the boardroom.

Says Stephen Hayklan, former chairman of the property company Wiggins Group plc: 'Being a non-executive director in a different type of business is of great stimulus to ideas when dealing with your own company's problems.'

Working in one company or sector it is very easy to forget that every business problem has been faced before somewhere else. Directors often worry unduly about particular problems because they do so in isolation believing that only close competitors face the same threats and challenges. Experience serving as an independent director can help directors lose their blinkers. For example, they quickly see that government legislation does not only affect their firm, and that many of the problems in their sector have already been successfully confronted elsewhere. You are no more likely to face a unique business problem than you are to face a unique medical disorder. The realization is valuable. It typifies the sort of thinking that distinguishes someone who has crossed the developmental threshold from executive to non-executive director.

Or, as Sir John Harvey-Jones puts it:[1] 'Seeing that things can be done in other ways causes one to question the practices "back at the ranch".'

Serving on someone else's board often provides opportunities as well to take part in exercises, such as acquisitions or dispositions, or raising capital on international markets, which do not normally arise in the company where you are an executive. When they do arise, however, the independent director has a specific and valuable experience (and useful contacts) that can enhance his or her contribution to the home board.

For example, Sir John Harvey-Jones[1] says he took his first non-executive directorship with Reed International for two reasons. Partly, he admits, because he was flattered to be asked, but also because Reed had a reputation as an acquirer of companies—rather as Hanson plc does today. He explains: 'I believed that acquisition of companies and disposal of parts of the group were skills which were little exercised inside ICI, but which would form an essential part of the armoury for the repositioning of our business in the future.'

Freedom to be creative

David O'Shaugnessy, a member of the supervisory board of CarnaudMetalbox, enthuses:

> The joy for me of the independent director position is that I am to be allowed real independence of thought for the first time. The role of an executive carries with it certain restrictions, which come from dependence on the company for a job. I don't think I will be tempted to surrender my new-found independence.
>
> It's a pleasure to be able to participate in the debate about the direction of the company without having to look over your shoulder at the chairman's view. Of course, that's also a frustration, because you can only participate in the debate through influence; you no longer have the executive power to make decisions and take action.

Our survey respondents gave very little importance to the financial aspects of their independent director positions. Their main motivations were opportunity to make a contribution, opportunity to learn and challenge.

One independent director echoes this mixture of frustration and emancipation. He explains:

> The chief frustration is that if you are used to doing it yourself, it's hard to remain hands-off. Often you feel you could do the job quicker yourself, but that is human arrogance. Overcoming that frustration is satisfying. When you see your ideas coming through and the company running well that is very satisfying.

Also, seeing younger people coming through is satisfying in the same way that it is for a father seeing his children doing well. The beauty of the independent director role is that you can get the satisfaction without all the hard work of running a company.

Christopher Weston, chairman of auctioneers, Phillips, has an amusing anecdote illustrating the need for empathy and understanding between independent and executive directors. As an independent director of Headline Book Publishing plc, he was checking that copies of that company's books were 'at eye level'. It was 5.15 a.m. at Gatwick Airport. There was a tap on his shoulder 'Would you mind leaving the stock alone, Sir?' He looked round slightly embarrassed. It was then that he saw Tim Hely Hutchinson, the MD of Headline, who was also travelling from Gatwick quite separately from Christopher Weston and had also been 'adjusting' the company's books so that they were at eye level.

Books are often impulse purchases and the two directors hoped that these actions would help sales.

WHY SUITABLE CANDIDATES DO *NOT* BECOME INDEPENDENT DIRECTORS

Equally important as an issue is why suitable people *do not* become independent directors. One of the reasons that the Great and the Good predominate among independent directors is because they are visible and obvious. By contrast, the pool of eligible candidates, who might offer a different perspective and experience, appears remarkably small and rarely obvious. This is especially true for women and racial minorities, from whom only a handful of people currently hold board posts on large quoted companies—and they are inundated with requests to join other boards as independent directors.

On the other hand, some very capable candidates do not get asked because people automatically assume they are too busy. Some of the most senior executives in the United Kingdom, who would be willing to serve, have never been approached.

Some well-qualified people do not become independent directors because they do not have the time. Says the chief executive of a major UK company: 'I won't take independent director positions because I believe my own company needs every minute I can spare for it. I can't afford to take my eye off the ball—that's the way to lose control.' An alternative view might be that this CEO runs the risk of being so internally focused that he and his top team will not be sufficiently sensitive to external change.

In a few cases, senior executives turn down independent director proposals on the grounds that the post is too modest, that they should only accept positions on companies of a similar or greater size as their own. Leaving aside the issue of self-importance, we would argue that this is short-sighted. Few people, who have proven themselves at board level in large organizations, need to keep on doing so—at least from a personal development point of view. The greatest value for someone at this level is likely to come from exposure to different situations, perhaps helping a young team with a new idea bring it to fruition.

John Ainley, of WH Smith (turnover £2 billion) joined the advisory board of the Priory Group of Hospitals (turnover £21 million) and found it enormously stimulating. He gained an overview into a variety of different functions, via a new sector. He found he knew more than he thought he did about business matters outside his own function, itself a pleasant and confidence-building exercise.

The independent director can transfer from being a leading executive director at one company to being an independent director on a subsidiary board of another, despite the different roles of the respective boards. Or such a person may move to a subsidiary which is larger than his or her own parent board of which he or she is a member.

Also, an independent director may sometimes feel more confident becoming an independent director if it is to a company which is related to his or her own area of expertise. Edward Weeks, a BASF director, joined the Babcock Contractors board with that reassurance. He quickly gained confidence. If there is a next time he will not specify a similar sector to his own.

WHAT BACKGROUND AND KNOWLEDGE SHOULD AN INDEPENDENT DIRECTOR BRING?

'The boardroom is no place for an amateur', says Richard Masterman,[3] an independent management consultant. Even less, he could have added, is it a place for the amateur independent director. The executive director normally at least has the benefit of approaching the board having been exposed to the politics of the organization for a reasonable period. His or her progress may well have been a direct result of understanding the politics of the organization. When the independent director steps on to the board, on the other hand, it is as if he or she passes from bright sunlight into a shuttered room: objects are visible, indistinctly, but it takes time for the eyes to adjust—time in which to trip over frayed carpets or walk into low-hanging light-fitments.

Clearly then, a period of grace is required for a new independent director to get up to speed. However, this should not stand in the way of using independent directors from a wider pool of expertise than that currently utilized.

The depressing uniformity of background of independent directors in most of the UK's top 500 companies is unlikely to stimulate a great deal of creative debate or the development of radically different strategic approaches, which many observers perceive as essential for economic growth.

However, Anne Spencer, author of *On the Edge of the Organization: The Role of the Outside Director*,[4] suggests that social fit is in itself seen as an important competence by independent directors. She explains:

> The board is seen as being a collection of very similar individuals and the non-executive director is seen as needing to share their (personal) characteristics, as a necessary part of competent role performance, without, at this stage, taking into account the non-executive director's technical competence to perform his role. His status as a competent member of the collectivity, whether the collectivity in question is defined as non-executive directors or as directors generally, is in the first instance heavily dependent simply on his similarity to his colleagues on a personal basis, on the basis, for instance of such criteria as class, educational background, social performance in terms of adeptness or otherwise. In

fact, as one, non-executive director interviewed expressed it: ' . . . that when a company is considering inviting in a non-executive director, there is, as it were, something of a club atmosphere situation . . . the question is asked: is he the sort of chap who will get on with us . . .?' Or, as more formally described: 'Collectivity-orientation, as it were, involves posing the "question of confidence", " . . . are you one of us or not? Your attitude on this question decides".'

If the non-executive director is too dissimilar from his colleagues then he is seen as simply being unable to perform his role in a satisfactory manner, and it is therefore impossible for him to satisfy any other criteria of competent membership.

What is wanted is someone who will 'fit in' with the collectivity comprising the board members: 'I think, socially adept to the norms of that particular board, without defining what you mean by socially adept.' In many of the interviews, it is suggested that since boardroom decisions are reached by consensus it is necessary that board members share, as it were, an initial consensus of basic cooperation, of understanding, to enable them to transact the affairs of the company, to make the decisions at which it is their function to arrive.

However, while it may make sense to seek executive directors with track records within the mould, it is becoming increasingly untenable to draw independent directors from such a narrow stratum of society. As an article in *The Financial Times* expressed it: 'The problem is not that suitable candidates do not exist, but that companies have too narrow a notion of the kind of person who would fit the role.' The same article lists five categories of would-be independent directors companies usually avoid: military men, academics, management consultants, bankers and retired people!

The range of potential candidates is greatly enlarged if the company looks at the professions. One of the largest law firms in the City, for example, has recently seconded two of its senior partners to large companies as non-executive directors. Lawyers, because of their commitment to professional ethics, often are ideally placed to provide independent advice and administer a restraining hand. That, at least, was behind the Law Society's call in 1979 for lawyers to become non-executive directors because they could offer independence and objectivity. Other professional societies, such as the Institute of Chartered Accountants also encourage members to seek independent director posts, although they are not permitted to join the boards of companies they audit. (Many managers might form the opinion, however, that there are already far too many accountants on British boards!)

The issue of broadening the selection criteria for independent directors is addressed in more detail in Chapter 6.

The independent director needs two distinct types of competence: generic competencies, which can be applied to any company, in which he or she acts as an independent director; and specific competencies relating to the individual company. These same divisions of competence apply equally well to any other senior position within a company. At a management level, the need to develop relevant skills is increasingly recognized, with expenditure rising annually. Initiatives such as the Management Charter Initiative have created a strong awareness of the development needs of senior managers.

At executive director level, the old assumption that having arrived was ample evidence that training was no longer necessary, is also disappearing fast. Although the proportion of UK main board directors with formal qualifications in direction is still very small, the Institute of Directors and institutions such as Henley Management College have experienced rapid expansion of their director development programmes.

All the more surprising then, that almost no training takes place for independent directors. In our recent survey[5] of non-executive directors, we asked what specific training they had received for this job. The universal response was none.

None the less, a strong minority (43 per cent) considered that some form of training was needed. The most common type of training suggested was some form of informal course, although some independent directors favoured a formal course leading to a qualification, shadowing of or mentoring by an experienced independent director, or some form of non-voting apprenticeship or observation at board meetings.

Does experience as an executive director automatically provide someone with the skills and capabilities to operate as an independent director? In our experience, generally not. As we saw in Chapter 2, the role of independent director is very different from that of executive director, so it would be surprising if the skills base *were* the same.

The skills an independent director needs will vary considerably according to the type of company, its current circumstances and prospects and the composition of the rest of the board. He or she may, for example, be required as a balancing factor, a facilitator, or as the grit in the corporate oyster. No independent director job exists in a vacuum: the independent director usually joins an existing team, composed of individuals with their own hidden agendas, strengths and weaknesses, and power bases. Learning to fit in can be a major task—equally difficult at one extreme, when the team is already very cohesive as at the other, when its members have failed to gel into a team at all.

Perhaps because of this diversity of role and circumstance, the handful of attempts that have been made to define competencies for independent directors have been largely anecdotal rather than based on any rigorous research. Masterman,[3] for example, points out that:

> Skills can be learnt by individuals and by the board as a whole. He selects six skills which he believes are important for the effective board of directors. *Creative insight* is asking the right questions, *sensitivity* is about listening, caring, communications, culture and behaviour patterns. *Vision* is the fusion of the first two in the process of anticipating change. *Versatility* is the response to the unexpected as the future unfolds and circumstances arise which were not in the vision. *Focus* is the concentration of the mind and the will and resources to implement change. Finally, *patience* is that vital skill which allows others to keep up with the board of directors. Time and space must be created by patience so that the firm can complete programmes of work before the mind of the firm moves on to new programmes.

Independent directors themselves also offer a range of suggestions:

Dr Brian Smith, independent chairman of BAA, perceives the key qualities to be:

> experience relevant to the job, and the courage of his convictions. The ability to persuade others is very important as an independent director can't tell people what to do. If the ability to influ-

ence is exercised well an independent director can be very effective, otherwise they will be ignored and ineffective. They have to have the courage of their convictions because at times it may be necessary to upset the whole applecart. Independent directors determine the ultimate succession and quality of the people running the company—that's their primary function.

Peter Sheldon, chairman of Stirling Group, suggests that the key qualities are: 'An open mind, patience, firmness when required, independence and a feel for the business of the company. The latter is indispensable. No amount of knowledge of finance or business generally will enable an independent director who does not have such a feel to make a contribution that will be valued by those who work in the company.'

If, as we would argue strongly, the competencies required of an independent director are as different from those of an executive director as the executive director's are from those of a senior manager, it may help to examine the latter. Author Colin Coulson-Thomas provides some useful insights.[6]

The qualities that distinguish directors from managers derive from their different legal duties and responsibilities and the role of the board. Directors require strategic awareness, the ability to see a company as a whole and understand the context within which it operates.

Not surprisingly, strategic awareness, objectivity, communication skills and the willingness to assume individual and collective responsibility rank high among the qualities sought in new appointees to the board. A degree of self-discipline may be needed to be an effective member of a boardroom team. There are particular roles in the boardroom such as chairman, chief executive or non-executive director that may require 'additional' skills beyond those possessed by other directors.

Directors differ from managers in their development needs. For example, they need to understand their particular accountabilities and duties, and the peculiar pressures, perspective and dynamics of the boardroom. The subtleties and distinct culture of the boardroom may take some time to absorb.

Reference has just been made to the qualities that distinguish between direction and management. In theory, the 'good director' should possess the attributes or quality of direction in greater measure. References to judgement, common sense, vision, wisdom, integrity, tact, etc., abound when chairmen are asked to describe the 'good director'.

Specifically, the ten most important qualities that separate direction from management, says Coulson-Thomas[6] (basing his conclusions on three surveys of directors) are:

- Strategic awareness and planning
- Objectivity—ability to see company as a whole
- Long-term vision
- Ultimate responsibility of company
- Commanding respect/leadership
- Decision-/policy making
- Anticipation of changing trends
- Delegation
- Lateral thinking
- Responsibility to shareholders

To these he adds ten qualities 'sought in directors of companies':

- Drive, determination, enthusiasm
- Loyalty and commitment
- Integrity
- Specialist knowledge
- Broad business understanding
- Presentation and communication skills
- Leadership
- Financial literacy and awareness
- Humour
- Intelligence/common sense

While most of the items on these two lists would apply equally to both executive and non-executive directors, some clearly do not. Delegation is not a core skill for an independent director—to whom would they delegate? Presentation skills are also of lesser importance (although other aspects of communication may be more important). And the degree of commitment that can reasonably be expected of an independent director will normally be different—indeed, it can be argued that too close an identification with the fortunes of the company on the part of the independent directors could be downright harmful!

While an ability to see the company as a whole is important, executive and non-executive directors cannot be expected to view it from the same perspective. The independent director will of necessity be standing a lot further back than the executives. Moreover, while the executive will often see the structure to a considerable extent in terms of personalities, the independent director will view it more in terms of logic and market fit.

Of course, most of the qualities in Coulson-Thomas's list can also apply equally well to senior managers. Indeed, the senior manager who lacks these qualities is likely to find it a significant hindrance to his or her chances of ever reaching the boardroom. The essential difference is one of *focus* and *degree*. Managers focus more on short- and medium-term objectives, on making strategies happen. Ideally, they should spend more of their time on planning and implementation than on formulating strategy and policy. Most of the focus of their efforts will also be internal, within the organization. External focus revolves mostly around customers. Directors, on the other hand, should concentrate their efforts on the longer term, on strategy and policy formulation, and on external relationships with influencing bodies such as government, the media and the investment community.

In practice, of course, the boundaries are greatly blurred. Many executive directors are also functional line managers, especially in smaller firms. Moreover, bitter experience has taught companies that creating strategies without the active participation of senior and middle management is of limited value—commitment is enhanced when the people, who have to implement strategies, feel some ownership for those strategies.

Coulson-Thomas[6] also provides a ranking of qualities directors considered very important in making new appointments to the board:

- Strategic awareness
- Objectivity
- Communication skills
- Individual responsibility
- Customer focus
- Self-discipline
- Team player
- Creativity
- Perspective
- Breadth

Our perception is that this list would be very different for appointments of independent directors. For example, the independent director will not take individual responsibility for any of the company's activities, other perhaps than in the capacity of chairperson of a board committee. He or she will certainly not be involved with the customers to any significant degree. While the independent director is a member of the board team, he or she will not be privy to the multitude of day-to-day interactions that make a close-knit executive team. A comparison might be a rugby team—the members of the scrum have to acquire a different kind of cohesion than the backs, but they are all part of the larger team and need to work well together.

Coulson-Thomas[6] also finds that the primary criterion used by chairmen to select managers for board positions is experience or track record. Functional expertise is not normally considered a strong factor, although presumably boards do try to maintain some form of balance. (Some of the classic company collapses have been where the board was heavily weighted with people from one discipline, such as engineering, R&D or marketing.)

In Table 3.1 we have drawn upon our own observation and upon interviews with independent directors and their executive board colleagues in an attempt to derive a more detailed comparison between all three types of job at the top of a company. In doing so, we recognize that many executives have the title director, but do not have a board role. We have classified these people (many of whom appear to have little

Table 3.1 The generic competencies needed by managers, executive directors and independent directors

Manager	Executive director	Non-executive director
Vision interpretation	Vision creation	Vision creation and testing
Strategy implementation	Strategic direction	Strategic perspective
Planning skills: interpretative	Directive	Stimulative
Leadership and followership	Leadership	Mentoring (counselling)
Problem-solving	Problem identification	Problem-probing
Team-building	Team-building	Team-nurturing
Creating power	Using power	Influencing without power
Finance: planning and budgeting	Financial policy-making and direction	Financial monitoring
Networking inside the organization	Networking inside and outside the organization	Networking mainly outside the organization
Project management	Project approval, evaluation and review	Project monitoring—relevance, probity, etc.
Controlling processes	Controlling results	Monitoring processes and results
Interpret and implement ethical guidelines	Establish ethical policy and guidelines	Ombudsman/ moral guardian—mediation
Communications: mainly to internal audiences	To internal and external audiences	Within the board: listening is as important as telling
Creativity in implementation	Creating the climate for creativity	Creativity through challenge and paradigm shift

© copyright Clutterbuck Associates.

idea of the potential responsibilities in law that go with adopting a grander title) simply as managers.

Let us look at these competencies in more detail.

Vision

A company that looks to its independent directors to provide vision and leadership has a real problem. Unless the chief executive is the main driver and creator of the corporate vision, there is very little chance that he or she will be able to play with conviction the missionary role that comes with the grand design. To live the vision, top management must own it, nurture it, caress it. Commitment comes because it is the child of their own imagination, experience and *Weltanschauung*.

What the independent director must do is challenge the vision, in a constructive way, helping shape and craft it by holding it up to the light and asking why? This demands a strong analytical capability, a capacity to absorb and sort out disparate clues, to step back and see the larger picture, and the interpersonal skills to question received wisdom without antagonizing the vision holders.

Strategy

Much the same competencies are required in handling the strategic dimensions. Essentially, strategy is a development of vision, a translation of vision into broad practical plans. The really effective independent director will invariably rely as much on instinct in assessing strategic approaches as upon analysis—indeed, he or she will rarely have time to follow the detailed analytical approaches that executive management should have followed. He or she will, however, detect where strategic analysis has been less than rigorous, demand explanations of how key conclusions were reached and contribute suggestions, based on previous experience and knowledge of what has been done elsewhere, to refine aspects of the strategy.

What the independent director should not do is become overly bogged down in the detail. A sign of an independent director out of his or her depth is a dogged insistence on following through a minor tactical issue, while missing the point on major strategic elements.

Recalls Clive Bastin: 'I know of some cases where an independent director had become so involved in the company in the detail that he was effectively taking on executive duties on behalf of the chairman or chief executive, and hence compromising his independence.'

Planning

Clearly, then, the independent director should not expect to participate closely in the development of implementation plans. He or she should, however, be prepared to be asked for advice on specific tactics, either where he or she has relevant experience of similar situations, or where there are broader policy considerations. For example, if a company, which has so far operated only in the United Kingdom, carries out work in France for a multinational customer, should it set up a permanent office there and seek other business to support it? The tactical issue of how best to service the customer has become bound up with the much more fundamental issue of when the company should go international itself.

The critical skill, then, is to recognize such situations and to bring the policy issues into focus when the executives become too close to see them.

Leadership

Independent directors have no one to lead, unless they occupy the chair. Nor, indeed, do they need the skills of followership, because they do not report to anyone, except the shareholders and that in the very broadest sense, but once a year.

What they do need to develop is the special skill of mentoring. The term comes from Greek mythology—when Ulysses set out on his epic voyage, he left his son in the hands of his trusted friend Mentor. Mentoring relationships involve the passing on of wisdom from an experienced, usually older person to a less experienced individual in what appears to be an unstructured, almost informal manner. It differs from teaching and tutoring, in that there is no syllabus or set course of learning to follow, and from coaching in that the majority of the learning is intuitive or tacit.

In practice, mentoring is a complex role composed of a number of management and interpersonal skills. Coaching does play a part, but a relatively minor one. Counselling is much more important, particularly in terms of helping the less experienced individual develop self-awareness and work through his or her own solutions to problems. Networking (of which more later) and facilitating (opening doors) are other important competencies of a mentor.

Most organized mentoring in the United Kingdom is targeted at graduate recruits and at junior managers. But mentors for directors and senior managers are becoming increasingly common.

The boards of the new National Health Trusts, for example, need rapid skills development to equip them to operate in a more commercial environment. One of the authors is a non-executive member of such a trust and has found the experience both rewarding and of great practical benefit. In the Oxford Regional Health Authority, these new directors are encouraged to find a mentor, who may be from inside or outside the region, and inside or outside the profession. Similarly, headmasters, who are increasingly being cast in the role of chief executive of schools, are also being encouraged to find mentors. An experienced governor, from a business background, can be an invaluable adviser and confidant(e).

When the independent director elects to play this role, he or she is essentially taking on the part of temporary godparent. In some cases, the mentor acts primarily as a wise counsellor, a confidant(e) able to provide a different perspective and help the executive to think issues through. In others, the executive has a clear need to learn the ropes of direction. Confiding fully in other board colleagues may be difficult, if not dangerous; the independent director offers a safe alternative.

A high proportion of mentoring relationships evolve into close personal friendships. Many also evolve into mutual supporting arrangements.

Effective mentors tend to be people who already have a reputation for developing others, whose knowledge is current, who command respect (but not awe), who are good listeners and have a sense of humour. Sometimes the latter characteristic is the most important of all!

Managing problems

One of the primary activities of executive management is to recognize problems and ensure that effective action is taken to resolve them. Independent directors simply do not have the day-to-day involvement or the depth of operational knowledge to play a major part in this process. What they should be able to do is to ask the questions (and demand answers) that oblige executives to look for problems in the right places.

Problems that are big enough to warrant board level discussion are worth intense scrutiny. The independent director has to have the skill to assess whether he or she is being given the whole problem, or just part of it; to relate the problem to what else he or she knows about the company to see if it can be aggregated into a larger problem capable of an integrated solution; and to challenge solutions that will merely paper over the cracks.

This requires more than mere perceptiveness. It often demands a dogged, courageous insistence on arriving at the right answer. (The difference between this and someone out of his or her depth lies in the relevance and scope of the questioning—in practice, it is rarely difficult to confuse the two.)

Non-executives have an important role in tackling the difficult issues which the executives tend to avoid. As John Hestlegrave, a non-executive director, describes it, they can be 'the nasty guys asking in a non-threatening way the turbulent questions which perhaps they were avoiding. Without creating a competitive environment they can get straight to what is right, not who is right.' He gives two examples of how this can work:

1. In one company the effects of deep recession were being felt. Different ways of organizing the workforce were discussed. By questioning, the non-executive directors discovered that the process would involve employees working part-time for over a year. They considered the effect on morale would be too destructive and that the company would have to bite the bullet and shed some people. 'It's sometimes hard', says Hestlegrave, 'to take a tough decision in a caring way'.
2. In another example, the executives were demonstrating a reluctance to rise to a challenge. The support of the non-executives helped to take the risk out of the necessary development. 'It is the role of the non-executives to enable people to be pro-active,' says Hestlegrave. 'Sometimes', he adds, 'an outsider can identify an interesting opportunity better than someone whose vision is concentrated inwards'.

Team-building

The main job of team-building lies with the chairman. But teams are composed of individuals prepared to subdue their individuality for a common purpose. All too often, independent directors, who are not quite sure what they are there for, pursue hobby-horses or hidden agendas of their own. Particularly in a highly politicized board, such people can be distinctly dysfunctional, providing few compensating benefits.

Being a team player is, by and large, a learned skill. People who have trained as professionals, operating largely independently, often have difficulty adapting to team-playing. So do many senior managers, used for too long to being top dog in their own areas of responsibility.

Effective team players recognize their own strengths and weaknesses, and those of the other team members. Rather than use this knowledge to score points or manipulate events, they use it to support colleagues and to know when to ask for and accept support themselves. Such behaviour requires a high degree of personal maturity, which may not always be present in the executive team in particular. Indeed, one of the key team-building roles of the independent director may be to support those executives who are less politically adept than their peers.

The variety of models of effective teams is wide, but most conclude that it is essential to maintain a balance between various types of personality—in particular, between people who get things done and people who think through implications of decisions. Of the nine personality types identified by Dr Meredith Belbin,[7] the least well regarded—yet often most valuable—is what he calls the team worker, who is efficient, personable and a good communicator, and who acts as the glue between the other team members. The role of the independent director may often be to act as a super team worker, helping the executive members of the board to focus more effectively on strategic issues, and fielding some of the more sensitive political issues in such a way that they are discussed without rancour.

The independent director may also act as what Belbin calls a 'plant'—an innovative thinker who stimulates discussion of new concepts, and forces the rest of the team out of mental ruts.

Power

Recent studies of how companies get things done have started to rehabilitate power as an important component of the corporate engine. While functional managers often have to invest time and effort into building the power structure that allows them to bring about change, executive directors, in theory at least, already have that power. Their problem is how to use it constructively. (It is a sad fact of life that a director passing through a department should beware of passing comment on anything that is not right, unless he or she considers it very important—almost invariably work in that department will stop for several days while everyone attempts to fix the problem, diverting attention from real priorities to attend to what may have simply been an observation of minor interest, or even just something to say!)

The independent director, however, has no real power (in practice, if not in law). Influencing skills—getting things done through persuasion, lobbying or sheer force of personality—are far more important.

Explains Clive Bastin: 'A successful independent director must be sufficiently aware of business and economic issues to contribute real added value to a discussion. Besides his skill competence he must show a canny understanding of the minds of business leaders, however entrepreneurial. A "poor politician" will find it very difficult to be an effective independent director.'

Financial competence

Financial competence is unfortunately often severely lacking at all levels of management. The independent director does not have to be a financial wizard, but he or she does have to be able to understand sufficient to challenge statements and to see behind the bald figures. If he or she is on the audit committee, then a much higher level of financial knowledge will normally be required.

Training in financial management is easily acquired—there are dozens of public courses, let alone internal company workshops. The key skills, however, can be summarized as follows:

- A basic understanding of how accounts are prepared and how to extract basic data on cash flow, profitability, margins and return on investment.
- A basic understanding of budgeting procedures (both generically and as they are applied within the particular company).
- Knowledge of what to look for when searching for common anomalies, hidden problems and individual projects or divisions, which are draining resources.

- The ability to relate the figures to the business plan and to medium-/long-term objectives.

Networking

If the value of the independent director lies primarily in the external view, which he or she is able to bring to the company, then the strength of his or her external networks is critical. In some cases, such as when the independent director is expected to be a channel to new business, these networks may be the most important value added.

However, to be truly effective, the independent director must supplement external connections with internal ones, not just at board level, but at a variety of other levels, too. If, for example, he or she is a functional specialist in his or her full-time employment, then it makes a lot of sense to get to know key people in that function within the company. The independent director will want a second source of information on the aspirations and ideas of people in the function (especially those ideas that do not make it to the board by formal routes). He or she will also value news about potentially serious problems being underplayed.

One of the essential skills in this situation is to be able to create relationships where people in the organization feel they can trust the independent director to maintain confidences. That demands that the independent director is sufficiently skilled in probing, to winkle out issues without appearing to have been prompted from below.

Another essential skill is to be able to use each 'node' of your network as a gateway to others. Persuading other people to open up their own networks takes time and a good deal of reciprocality—yet the independent director is constrained from being the source of much information, by the need to maintain confidentiality in the boardroom. Managing this cobweb of obligations and allegiances is difficult enough for the manager, who works full-time in the organization, but for the independent director it requires an even higher level of skill—especially if he or she is to avoid being seen as overtly political.

Project management

One of the classic scenarios of corporate collapse is the organization that takes on the grand project. Either the project is beyond its resources (financially, technologically or in the competence of its people), or it is unsoundly based. In the latter case, so much top management commitment has gone into getting the project off the ground that anyone who suggests it should be abandoned or at least re-evaluated is immediately classed as negative or unconstructive.

The independent director should have enough knowledge of project management principles to ask the right questions about major projects (which we would define as any project that absorbs more than 10 per cent of a company's key resources). Is it on track in terms of schedule and cost? If there are overruns, how are they being tackled? What would the comparative costs be of withdrawing versus carrying on? What lessons can we learn to apply to future large projects?

Most of these questions should, of course, be asked by the executive directors. But all too often they may be too close to the issue—especially if they are the sponsors of the project—to be fully objective in their answers. The independent director has to be able to maintain the dogged pursuit of reality.

Davy Corporation, for example, suffered from a substantial project that got out of hand. Trafalgar House bought Davy and Davy's problems subsequently turned out to be so bad that they indirectly led to the downfall of Sir Nigel Broackes and the unwelcome arrival as shareholders of the HongKong Land Company.

Process control

By and large, the multiplicity of processes and procedures a company carries out to achieve its objectives are the business of senior management. The board is primarily interested in results. None the less, some processes may be so important that they warrant a strong monitoring presence at board level and this will often be provided by bringing in an independent specialist. For example, customer service is so important in the retail world that it pays to create an ombudsman position, preferably filled by an independent director, who will have greater credibility than a full-time employee of the company.

Ethical management

The requirement for the board to maintain the ethical climate of the organization will become increasingly important. The independent director has a special role to play here—he or she is essentially responsible for monitoring and reviewing the ethical behaviour of the executives. (This may not be strictly so in law, but it is an increasingly common expectation of shareholders and the general public.)

To fulfil that obligation, the independent director needs an understanding of why and how ethical dilemmas arise; how to identify situations when ethical dilemmas are most likely to occur; and how to analyse and resolve resulting conflicts of interest. Without this understanding, it is very difficult to make a case against an unethical behaviour or policy. Ethical issues need to be reduced to the rational level before they can be discussed in a meaningful way.

The capability of leading or facilitating such discussions and achieving consensus, based on clear ethical principles is very valuable. Indeed, boards which cannot exercise this kind of discipline will increasingly put their reputations at risk.

The independent director should also have sufficient grasp of best practice in this complex area to ensure that the company has policy guidelines on all key social issues affecting the business, and that these are reviewed from time to time. He or she should also be able to monitor and review how well those policies are being implemented.

Communications

The internal communications role of the independent director is usually very limited, at least in terms of giving information—he or she should not normally be seen to be doing the executives' job. Much the same is true of external communications, where audiences look to the chairman (executive or non-executive) and CEO as the prime ambassadors for the company. This is slowly changing, with more and more companies involving independent directors in presentations to investment funds and on public platforms. If this trend continues, presentation and public speaking skills will become more important for the independent director.

The most important communications role for an independent director, however, is within the boardroom itself. Although he or she may have been selected for the personal wisdom and experience that can be passed on, in practice, the key communications skill is listening. The independent director needs to be able to absorb a great deal of information, filling in the gaps between what is said by the executives and what the executives wrongly assume the other board members already know. The independent director needs to respond in such a way that critical comments are seen as positive and naïve questions are seen as probing. He or she needs to be able to summarize arguments, as much for the benefit of others around the table as for personal gain. And he or she needs to make critical points forcefully, succinctly and intelligibly without appearing to dominate the meeting.

Anecdotal evidence suggests that the quality of communications within most boardrooms is relatively poor. Anything the independent director can do to enhance both written and spoken communications at board meetings must be of considerable value. After all, if the company cannot communicate effectively at the top, how can it expect to get key messages down to the shopfloor, let alone receive them back?

Creativity

For a senior manager, creativity may in fact be an impediment to promotion to the board. The problem is that directors, who have few ideas themselves, can fear or resent people who are prolific innovators. Moreover, in practice, an executive director does not need to be a highly creative thinker—merely someone who is able to stimulate creativity in others, and able to recognize a good idea when he or she sees one. Highly creative executives usually need to be balanced by other team members, who have their feet firmly on the ground.

Independent directors, however, typically should provide a valuable dose of creative thought. Even if they are not creative individuals, they should be able to draw on experience to present substantially different ways of looking at problems. It is important in this context that independent directors do not restrict their contribution simply to their own areas of expertise. In most cases, independent directors find they know more than they think about other areas because of their experience on the board of their own company. Quite simply, the knowledge of colleagues rubs off and can be used effectively to ask and ask again. Such questioning not only does the board good, but is also very valuable for the individuals who become better all-rounders. Essentially, independent directors will stimulate creativity at board level by:

- challenging why things are always done in a particular way ('controlled *naïveté*' is a valuable technique here);
- drawing parallels with other organizations that do things differently;
- posing 'what if' questions, based on radically different scenarios of the future;
- testing alternative assumptions (playing Devil's advocate).

Independent directors may not have all these competencies at the start, but the sooner they acquire them, the more effective they will be—not just on the host board but in their main employment as well.

On top of the generic competencies lies the whole stratum of situation-specific competencies—those essential for a good fit into the particular board team. These will normally relate to one or more of the following:

- *Function*: for example, marketing or R&D. Typically, the independent director will provide additional expertise. As we saw in Chapter 2, the added value should come not from substituting for the role of the functional specialist (for example, if a company needs marketing direction, it should be executive direction) but for particular expertise within the function. In essence, the effective independent director in this role becomes a confidant(e) and support for the relevant functional executive.

Competence here is largely a function of reputation and experience.

- *Sector*: the independent director may have specific knowledge of the host company's industry; or of new sectors, into which the company is moving.

  Again, competence derives largely from the relevance and depth of previous experience.

- *New situation*: when a company is at a crossroads in its development, it helps to have someone who has been there before. Typical areas of expertise might include previous participation in a management buy-out, international expansion or acquisition, or privatization.

  Competence in this case derives from either frequency or intensity of experience.

- *Scope*: where the independent director offers insights into another dimension, e.g. internationally, or in a broader spread of industry.

  Competence comes from the ability to transfer broad experience into specific practical insights.

- *Personal networks*: where the independent director retains strong links with customers, suppliers or other major influencers of the business's fortunes—former civil servants or army officers are common. For example, retired senior armed forces personnel can be found on the boards of defence industry companies such as GEC, Racal or Plessey.

  Competence comes from being able to maintain these networks in a healthy state; from developing them rather than allowing them to atrophy, as normally happens.

- *Direction*: experience of other boards. Most independent directors will automatically have this expertise.

  Competence comes from the ability to learn from these experiences and use them to enhance the performance of the host company board.

- *Temperament*: strong personal characteristics, such as

drive, creativity or, alternatively, the ability to bring down to earth a visionary chief executive.

The characteristic is in effect a competence in its own right. However, great care must be exercised to ensure that it is not taken to extreme—strong personality traits can often become counterproductive if they are not controlled.

Measuring the independent director's contribution

Given the broad range of involvements an independent director may have with a company, it is not easy to define a generic set of measurements, which enable shareholders and executives to judge their worth. However, it should be a standard part of the appointment process to devise with a newly appointed independent director just how his or her performance will be evaluated. Apart from anything else, this helps both parties focus on useful outcomes. This is an issue we will explore in more detail in the next chapter, but some broadbrush measurements that can be applied include the following:

- Contribution to establishing strategic direction.
- Type and extent of alternative experience he or she is able to bring to bear on discussions.
- Influence on key decisions.

These are all 'soft' measurements, but they have the advantage of making executives think through how they are using the independent directors.

Once you have effective and agreed measurements, it becomes possible to remove one of the main differences between executive and non-executive directors—incentives based on performance. Why, ask some independent directors, should executives be rewarded for good performance when we are not? On the other hand, who decides what is a fair incentive? After all, the main advantage of having independent directors on the remuneration committee is that they do not benefit from its decisions.

SUMMARY

If nothing else, we hope this chapter has demonstrated that the role of independent director is far from the simple one that is so often assumed. It demands an understanding of both practical problems facing the host business and the politics within it. The would-be independent director should not expect to be able to make a significant contribution by simply turning up to board meetings. To give real value to the company he or she must become sufficiently involved to gain and impart genuine understanding.

The independent director must know enough about the company to understand the complexity of its business and markets, but be sufficiently detached to retain an independent view.

REFERENCES

1. Sir John Harvey-Jones, *Making it Happen: Reflections on Leadership*. Collins, 1988.
2. Tom Nash, The growing power of non-executive directors. *The Director*, September 1989.
3. Richard Masterman, Comments on Creating an Effective Board. Presented at the IPM National Conference 1991.
4. Anne Spencer, *On the Edge of the Organization: The Role of the Outside Director*. Wiley, 1983.
5. Making the most of Non-Executive Directors—a survey by Hanson Green and the ITEM Group plc, 1992.
6. Colin Coulson-Thomas, Competent directors: boardroom myths and realities. *Journal of General Management*, **17**(1), Autumn 1991.
7. Dr Meredith Belbin, *Management Teams: Why They Succeed or Fail*. Heinemann, London, 1981.

4 How can independent directors contribute more?

In this chapter we have tried to set out some guidelines to help independent directors contribute effectively. For most, there will be a steep learning curve at the start of their relationship with a new company. In some cases, too, the first few months will involve a crash course in a new sector or industry. While it is to be hoped that they will have been selected for their own talents and business backgrounds— which are in effect the stars by which they will steer in the new role—the more assistance and information they can get from the company itself, the sooner they can put the picture together and begin to add value. Clearly, too, it is in the interests of the company making the appointment to give all the assistance and support it can to allow an individual to contribute fully in the role of independent director.

INDUCTING THE INDEPENDENT DIRECTOR

We recommend a structured approach to induction (as with other senior positions). However, as short-sighted as it may seem when weighed against the value they can potentially add to the company, our research suggests that unless newly appointed independent directors are prepared to fight for a good induction they are unlikely to get it.

The 38 independent directors who responded to our survey[1] in detail had a very mixed experience in terms of induction. In their first choice or main independent director post, 32 had a meeting with the chairman and 20 had meetings with other directors. Only five had meetings with a representative sample of other employees in the company; 24 received some written materials about the company, with 11 companies sending copies of previous board minutes. Site visits were arranged for 14 of them. Not one attended the formal induction and orientation programme that normal employees would be given, nor did they receive even a truncated version of it.

For those respondents with second and third independent director positions, the same general proportions were reflected.

Anecdotal evidence would also suggest that induction of independent directors is frequently ill-planned and poorly executed. 'Many independent directors do not know enough about the business they should be advising on,' commented one experienced independent director.

Often, too, the induction period sets the tone for how the appointment works in practice. A scarcity of information at the outset, for example, creates a low expectation of the contribution required. Quite simply, the extent to which the independent director is inducted into the company's culture and business impacts directly on his or her effectiveness.

'The amount of information a non-executive director gets is much more important than it used to be. As an independent director, I want to know what is going on in areas such as safety where I have a legal responsibility,' observed one independent director.

Best practice in independent director induction appears to involve the following:

- A clear contract and covering letter, as detailed in Chapter 5.
- Time with other executive directors (in particular, the chairman, the company secretary and, if the independent director is a functional specialist, his or her executive counterpart).
- A copy of previous board minutes for at least the past six months, with explanation of the background behind them.
- A copy of the business plan, together with profiles of the key competitors and their strategies.

- A copy of any recent significant reports by management consultants on areas of board responsibility.
- An opportunity to attend board meetings as an observer before the appointment is confirmed.
- An opportunity to attend other key management meetings.
- An opportunity to attend presentations to the investment community.
- Visits to key sites (including overseas locations, if the business is strongly international).
- Introduction to some key customers and suppliers.
- Invitations to company social events, such as sponsored concerts.
- A formal 1–2 day induction programme, including many of the elements above, but also presentations from various divisions on their strengths, weaknesses and ambitions.
- Appointment of a mentor, from among the more experienced independent directors on the board, for the first few months.

The objective is to give the independent director a rapid and unconfusing insight into the company, without making him or her so familiar with its operations that he or she no longer feels able to ask naïve questions. It helps in this process if each of the individuals involved has a clear brief of what information he or she is intended to pass on. The chairman/ CEO should focus on broad strategic objectives and to a lesser extent on the politics of the organization. The company secretary should focus on the conduct of the board meetings and the interaction between key players, both at board meetings and in day-to-day operations. Functional executives should focus on their own areas of responsibility. Existing independent directors should provide a general overview of the organization as they see it—preferably without trying to impose their views on the newcomer, part of whose value is that he or she comes with a whole different set of perspectives. The formal induction should attempt to breathe life into the annual report and business plan.

Such an intensive induction will only happen if the

independent director is prepared to give up the time and if it is efficiently organized. Although it is ultimately the chairman's/CEO's responsibility, it will normally be delegated to another executive, most often human resources or the company secretary. The seriousness with which the company tackles the induction programme is a very good and public indication of how seriously it values its independent directors.

Finally, some executive directors, and even the occasional shareholder, argue that it is wrong for an independent director to have a vote equal to that of the executive director, being only an independent and at best only partially familiar with all aspects of company policy. But this misses the point. An effective and appropriately selected independent director is able to make decisions purely on their commercial merits, without taking personal aspirations into account. His or her vote, therefore, is certainly worth the same in practice.

WHAT CAN THE COMPANY DO TO TRAIN INDEPENDENT DIRECTORS?

Clearly, it is in the best interests of the company that its independent directors should be able to contribute rapidly and substantially to strategic decision-making. Where the company provides no training, it effectively devalues the independent director position and promotes the suspicion that independent directors have been appointed more for form than for substance.

There are two basic situations, in which the host company should offer training to independent directors. The first assumes that the individual is already an experienced non-executive, having served on several boards in this capacity before. How much the individual will have learnt depends upon his or her own capacity for absorbing and internalizing experience and the particular circumstances of the boards in question. It is fully possible for someone to have held a number of independent director posts and still be ignorant or incompetent on some of the essentials.

So, for the experienced independent director, it is important to discuss at an early stage what kind of training or support might be helpful. Defining precisely what situation-specific competencies will be required enables the company to examine with independent director candidates how well their experience matches the 'fit' required. It also opens up the possibilities to offer 'refresher' training in areas, where the independent director may feel lacking. For example, many senior managers will never have acquired some of the creativity management skills that can be essential when discussing complex strategic issues. Equally, an independent director might well find it valuable to acquire a rapid knowledge of the industry, if it is relatively new ground. Approached in the right way, even the most senior people will normally respond well. If they respond badly, this can be taken as an indication of a closed mind, or of a dangerous obsession with personal status, both of which could prove damaging to the proper functioning of the board.

What so often happens, when a senior figure is approached to join the board as an independent director, is that both sides are too embarrassed to raise the subjects of competence and training. What is essentially a failure of courage and frankness on both sides can give rise to major problems later.

The second situation is where the candidate does not have previous experience as an independent director. Again, this situation can be subdivided, this time into people who have had executive board positions (or preferably are currently employed as a full-time executive director), and senior managers being groomed for board level positions. Clearly, the latter will normally need greater exposure to learning opportunities than the former. However, the nature of training and development is likely to be much the same—not least because many of the executive directors will have received no formal training for their jobs either.

A comprehensive training programme for an independent director might include the following elements:

- A formal course in the duties and responsibilities of directors in general.
- Mentorship by a more experienced independent director, preferably, but not necessarily on the same board. (The

mentor can contribute more to his or her protégé(e)'s development if there is an opportunity to observe the protégé(e) in action.) One option rarely if ever applied is for potential independent directors to be assigned to mentors, who will take them along to board meetings they attend as independent directors. This requires the cooperation and trust of the host company, of course.

- A formal personal development plan constructed to address those competencies, where the individual is relatively weak. For example, he or she could enhance strategic skills by being assigned to a working party to develop strategic options for part of the business.
- Exposure to similar roles in other contexts. For example, he or she might be seconded to the governing board of a charity on the company's behalf, or to the trustees of a pension fund. The variety of such organizations is expanding rapidly, with hospital trusts, school governorships, enterprise agencies and Training and Education Councils all seeking senior managers to join their boards.

At the time of writing there does not exist a formal qualification in independent direction, although there are diplomas in direction in general. Unfortunately, much of the content of these diploma courses is largely irrelevant to the non-executive role. Given the difference in the two roles, this is a major gap. Some public workshops on corporate governance, such as the one day programme run by Sundridge Park,[2] contain a strong element of independent director issues—but these are a rarity in Europe. The Sundridge workshop is based on the concept of board engineering—the idea that the board should be designed and that the individuals should make up a team. It takes as its starting point that the directors as a whole are responsible for:

- vision and strategy;
- measuring and monitoring performance;
- making sure key appointments and organizational structure are right ... but that executive action should be in the hands of the executives.

Much of the value of this approach is that executives and independent directors attend together and can develop understanding together.

Of course, the independent director should not expect someone else to provide the training he or she needs. As with any other vocation or activity, competence can be acquired in a variety of ways. John Harper, head of professional development at The Institute of Directors, provides a useful analysis, which is as applicable to independent as to executive directors (see Table 4.1).

Table 4.1   *Training methods for the independent director*

Method	Knowledge	Skills	Awareness	Experience
Courses	x	x		x
Learning by doing	x	x		x
Conferences	x	x	x	x
Workshops	x	x	x	x
Personal development groups	x	x	x	x
Recorded tapes	x		x	
Books	x		x	
Newspapers and TV	x		x	
Journals	x		x	
Counselling	x			

MEASURING EFFECTIVENESS

At most levels in the well-run company there is frequent measurement of the output of both teams and individuals. In most companies, however, the process of measurement stops firmly at the boardroom door. Coulson-Thomas[3] found that only one in eight companies 'operates any form of periodic and formal appraisal of performance in the Boardroom'.

One reason for this is perhaps that the company is unclear exactly what it should be looking for in terms of results. Whereas it is usually relatively easy to judge a manager on whether or not he or she has achieved annual targets, a director's input is more subtle and will frequently have its impact over a number of years. Another reason may well be that directors do not have the personal courage to expose themselves to assessment in this way.

An alternative explanation comes from John Cheele,[4] a business consultant, who holds four independent directorships, who was reported in *The Director* as saying: 'Most research and writing on the subject of non-executives has tended to duck the issue of effectiveness, because it is so difficult to come up with anything ... You can't measure a non-executive's performance if you do not have a precise idea of what it is you want him to do.'

Although the criteria for assessing the input of independent directors may of necessity have to be 'soft', they should none the less be rigorously applied—if for no other reason than to permit the independent director to understand how his or her contribution is perceived. The discussion on adding value in Chapter 2 should provide some starting points for agreeing measurements of performance. In the end, however, any assessment must be largely subjective. As Steve Shirley, founder director of FI Group expresses it: 'Non-executive directors are judged as people, not by their deeds.'

Bob Tricker, professor of finance and accounting at the University of Hong Kong, suggests that non-executive directors should appraise themselves using a matrix that shows the effectiveness in each role against the importance of that role within the particular board. For this kind of self-appraisal to be useful, we would recommend that the independent director first agree with board colleagues what the roles are and which in their view are most important. The astute questioner will no doubt glean without asking some measure of how effective they think he or she is in each role.

The same kind of matrix can be used to assess each of the skills or competencies in terms of importance and effectiveness. Clearly, any scores low on both axes can be ignored in terms of impact on the job, as can any that indicate low importance and high effectiveness. But any that are both important to the board and an area of weakness in contribution should stimulate discussion and remedial action.

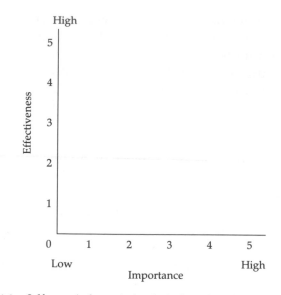

Figure 4.1   *Self-appraisal matrix for the independent director*

As would be the case with any other person working with the company, the discussion of performance should result in an action plan, even if that is simply to continue as before. If a problem is highlighted, then a solution should be worked out jointly. That solution may involve training, increased access to key individuals or information, greater availability of time, or, in extreme cases, an agreement to part company.

In cases, where independent directors have been pushed to resign, it is usually very difficult to identify precisely where they have failed. Indeed, in many instances, the suspicion remains that they have been forced out because they were too effective in challenging executive management.

The most difficult issue is who should appraise the independent director. Theoretically, at least, it should be the chairman, on the grounds that his or her performance is judged by the shareholders. From a practical point of view, however, this could pose serious problems in a company where the independent directors do not fully support the chairman.

The key to this dilemma lies, we believe, in recognizing that the board is essentially a team of people who share responsibility towards the organization's stakeholders; so it should be the team who makes judgements on performance. A variety of techniques exist to help with this process. These will mostly involve confidential feedback to a trusted third party who will build a composite picture and discuss it with each director on a one-to-one counselling basis.

Because the independent director is joining a team (or at least a grouping of individuals with the potential to become a team) the actual role he or she plays will to a considerable extent be shaped by the preconceptions of the other board members. It is only human nature to respond to other people's expectations. Certainly, we would advise anyone considering taking up a post as an independent director to meet *all* the other directors beforehand, to ask basic questions such as:

- What do you think the independent director role should be in this company?
- Do you genuinely see a need for the post?
- What kind of help would you most value from an independent director and why?
- What would you *not* want an independent director to do?

It also helps to be clear in your own mind about the differences between a manager and a director, and between an executive and a non-executive director. If you can check that your intended board colleagues share your understanding of the differences, so much the better.

The transition between senior manager and director is a subtle and often underrated one. The shift in thinking patterns demands a change in perspective. Issues need to be considered from the longer term; corporate reputation assumes a higher importance in decision-making; the interaction between internal functions and between the organization and its external partners takes on a new and broader context. In essence, the role of the director is to determine policy; that of the manager to interpret and turn policy into action. Given that so many directors get this wrong, it is perhaps not surprising that independent directors often also have some confusion.

Colin Coulson-Thomas,[3] who has made a particular study of this issue, describes the difference in this way:

> The qualities that distinguish directors from managers derive from their different legal duties and responsibilities and the role of the Board. Directors require strategic awareness, the ability to see a company as a whole and to understand the context, in which it operates. Formulating a distinctive vision and a realistic strategy requires objectivity and the ability to look ahead. A vision and strategy has also to be communicated and shared

J. Beevor, an international lawyer and financier, offered an alternative perspective—though not a contradictory one. Writing in 1979,[5] he said the role of a director is essentially advisory and supervisory even though many of these processes lead to executive action. The board as a whole, he says, has one supreme executive act to perform which is to hire or fire the chief executive, into whose hands the management of the company is entrusted. In almost all its other activities the board of directors is advisory to the chairman or chief executive and supervises both the performance of management and the periodical revision of policy and organization. While, as Beevor himself admitted, this description sounds somewhat idealistic when compared to the average board meeting, it nevertheless provides a useful perspective on the role of all directors, and in particular the independent director.

Directors also differ from managers in their development needs, Coulson-Thomas points out. There is much less emphasis on functional know-how than on broadening perspective and understanding the peculiar dynamics and culture of the boardroom. It is not surprising, therefore, that companies such as Trafalgar House Construction have used a mixture of formal and informal training for senior managers with the potential to join subsidiary boards. The informal elements of the director development process involve mentoring relationships, where intuitive learning can take place. This approach recognizes that many of the key skills a director needs cannot easily be written down or taught in a classroom. They involve tacit knowledge, which is largely absorbed by observation, association and direct experience. However, the Mumford Report in the late 1980s found that the vast majority of directors receive no training at all.

Although there is legally no difference between executive and non-executive directors (the legal responsibilities are explained in detail in Chapter 5), there are several common differences in what they do and how they are rewarded. Among them are the following

- *Time commitment.* On average an executive director will work 60 hours a week for the company; the independent director 60 hours a year.
- *The ambassadorial role.* Executive directors will normally focus their communications internally; independent directors will address primarily external audiences. The exception is the combined chairman/chief executive, who is expected to communicate the strategic vision to both. Where the role of chairman and CEO is split, the CEO normally concentrates on the internal audience and the chairman on the external.
- *Incentives.* Executive directors are usually given incentives such as share options and/or performance bonuses; independent directors usually are not. This is an issue of increasing contention, however, not least because the independent director shares the same risks to his or her reputation if the company's performance is poor. We expect to see the development of tailored incentive schemes aimed at independent directors.
- *Golden handshakes.* Again, compensation for dismissal has become a commonplace element of executive contracts, but is rare for non-executives. Yet the independent directors are usually the first victims of a takeover.
- *Most executive directors are also managers.* Coulson-Thomas[3] reports that 'When asked how they split their time between directorial roles most directors claim to allocate between a quarter and a third to direction and the remainder to managing their divisions or departments.' This dual role gives the executive director much greater influence on what happens in the organization—the policies that get implemented are those that the executives put their weight behind.
- *Accommodation.* Non-executives, other than non-

executive chairmen, do not normally have an office in the company. There are, of course, some exceptions, especially where the independent director is a former executive director.

Some observers suggest that the differences between executive and non-executive directors should all be swept away. For example, executive search company Merton Associates, which surveyed 268 independent directors in 1991,[6] advocated the substitution of the 'legally defined part-time director':

- who would have executive responsibility for ensuring that the policy of the company is executed
- whose powers are seen as no less than those of other full time directors
- who has specific responsibilities for discharging a fiduciary role in a listed company
- who will still retain his/her essential independence by remaining outside the company's management, and who will not become, *per se*, an employee of that company.

Our own opinion is that this would undermine some of the main benefits of an independent director, not least because it would narrow the scope of his or her potential contribution. However, the debate will undoubtedly continue and different companies will find different solutions.

A further influence on how the independent director role is cast will often come from how the board sees itself creating value, and who the value is being created for.

In that context it is useful to consider the primary duties and responsibilities of the board. At its simplest, says Brian Smith:

The first job of the board is to ensure that the company is managed properly today.

The second job of the board is to be concerned with where the company is going. That's where an independent director can play a more positive role than just that of policeman. They can't get involved with the day to day management of the company, but they can have an important impact on strategy issues.

A more comprehensive description appeared in the *Harvard Business Review* in November 1976. As summarized in a speech by J. Beevor,[5] directors are responsible:

- Primarily to shareholders, with a secondary responsibility (sometimes overriding the first) to employees, creditors and the community. Directors should continually keep in mind the security of investment and dividend policy and the return on investment.
- For selecting and appointing the chief executive and delegating all duties of management not specifically reserved to the board. They are responsible, too, for considering—especially when making that appointment—the question of future succession.
- For reviewing and appraising the performance of the chief executive in the execution of his duties, and that of each executive department head, both annually in relation to their plans and budgets, and at shorter intervals if necessary.
- For reviewing major corporate objectives, policies and budgets proposed by the chief executive; and approving all major projects such as entering a new line of business or abandoning an old one, plus mergers, etc.
- For reviewing at least annually the financial structure of the company, including limits of short-term debt, maintenance of a margin of short-term borrowings to meet contingencies, and possibilities of long-term funding.
- For reviewing board organization, including size, age limits, remuneration, and the system of board committees.
- For supervising management, including the duties of the chief executive, plans for succession, reports, emoluments and development.
- For reviewing employee relations, including pensions, profit-sharing, and other benefit plans.
- For approving auditors and primary legal advisers and others (and reviewing the system of audit committees).
- For serving individually as advisers to the chairman and chief executive, and with their approval, to their officers.

- For ensuring that the company complies with all relevant national, international and foreign laws.
- For reviewing annually this statement of duties, and considering any proposals for changes to it.

Among all this detail, it is important of course not to lose sight of the value an effective board of directors can add to an organization.

Ada Demb and Friedrich Neubauer, professors at IMD in Switzerland, identify three main areas in which such value may be added:[7]

1. *Auditing and monitoring executive management.* Simply having someone to report to on a regular basis can be very helpful in making executives think through what they are doing and why. Justifying actions within a context of taking a variety of stakeholder interests into account promotes more rigorous analysis. The board is only one of the auditors of management, of course (the Stock Market, credit rating agencies, legislators and others all look critically at performance), but it is the closest to the point where policy decisions are made.
2. *Strategy review.* An annual strategic review is becoming more common, say Demb and Neubauer. Such reviews have several advantages, they claim, including:
   (a) Helping independent directors 'move along the learning curve of the industry'. It can take two or three years, they suggest, before 'intelligent and critical judgement can be exercised about the company, its subsidiaries and operating locations can be exercised at board level.
   (b) Scrutinizing management proposals from a broader perspective.
   (c) Enabling independent directors to react more rapidly and with greater forethought when sudden acquisition opportunities arise. 'Given adequate background, Board members tell us they are willing and able to respond quickly and supportively to fast-moving developments between meetings.'
   (d) Developing independent director commitment to strategic plans.

(e) Improving the quality of board decision-making in selecting a new chairman and/or chief executive.

3. *Corporate governance.* 'Someone must choose the external standards, to which the corporation must respond. This is a role for the board,' say Demb and Neubauer ... 'The issue here is not compliance. Only management has the technical knowledge to develop systems, which ensure compliance ... the board can identify those boundaries, where value judgements will be required—those fences reflecting standards set by "industry practice", "company philosophy" or "ethical norms".' Essentially, this should provide the answer to 'who is the company creating value for?' The public perception that ethical standards have fallen in business plus the observations of the Cadbury Committee, will increase the importance of this role.

In summary, they conclude, 'The value the board can add to the corporation stems from the breadth and independence of judgement that can be exercised by a group of experienced professionals who are, themselves, removed from direct operational responsibility. Only at the board level can the corporation achieve a true 360 degree perspective of its activities—a comprehensive and synthetic view of its business.

The model of the board, on which these two academics base their conclusions, is essentially that of Continental Europe, where independent directors form most if not all of the board membership. Within the structure of a British board there can be a much wider range of composition. Typically, among smaller companies in particular, the executives will form a majority. The same potential to add value will apply, but may be constrained by the inability of executives to step out of their operational roles and take a directorial perspective. Demb and Neubauer's conclusions tend to add weight to the argument that the balance of a UK board should be tipped towards the independent directors.

United Kingdom boards are frequently too large to be effective. While there should be an adequate representation of independent directors, too many increases the quantity of discussion at the expense of quality.

There are plenty of stories about the optimum size of an effective organization, or, in this case, of a board. Jesus chose only 12 Apostles and in the eighteenth century Great Britain ruled both Canada and India with about a dozen civil servants. However, in the business context, the independent directors who flourish say almost invariably that a board of over 15 is too cumbersome. Nor should there be a need for greater numbers if one is clear about the role of the board itself. The board should not, and cannot, represent all constituents. The smaller the board, the less likely it is that the chairman will be able to pack it with contacts, or allow the board to become a depository for former employees, a retirement home. For example, we would contend—and most independent directors would agree—that Prudential's board is both too large and wrongly composed, having too many former directors.

Veteran independent director Sir Lewis Robertson supports the view that independent directors should always be plural, explaining: 'A single external director at a board otherwise consisting entirely of executive directors cannot make the full and effective contribution to the company's life: his opinions as he expresses them become personalised and are received not as those of a detached grouping of people, but of Jack or Tom.' The collective independent opinion, he believes, is what carries real weight with the executive team.

Various surveys of Britain's largest companies suggest that most companies have some form of independent directors, with banks, building societies, oil companies, television companies and recently privatized groups having the largest numbers. A study by Arthur Andersen in 1992[8] found that 90 per cent of 1612 large companies surveyed had some form of non-executive representation on the board. Over 80 per cent had between one and five independent directors.

Companies, which have only a small proportion of independent directors, often have the assumption that independent directors will make their main contribution to value creation through some form of specialist expertise. This can be a very myopic approach, preventing the independent director from becoming deeply involved in strategy development, or from challenging executive behaviour as forcefully as might be the case if the role were interpreted more broadly. Sir Lewis Robertson, again, has some strong words on the subject, advising against

> using the non-executive directors to fill clear gaps in a company's skills portfolio. If a company needs marketing, say, and is weak in this, the need is a management rather than a board-level one. But there should be relevancy of experience; for instance, in a construction company, exposed to long-period contracts with their financing, cost and legal risks, then the presence among externals of some sort of long-contract experience (from another sector) would be useful. Experience should be such as to give the right mental approach, but need not be and mostly should not be direct.

More important than sector experience (which will tend to reside among competitors, the retired or consultants, none of whom, in most cases, make particularly suitable independent directors) in value creation is how well the board team works together. As an outsider joining the team, the independent director needs to have a good fit, from the point of view of personality, weight and status, and simple chemistry with the rest of the members. Getting the balance of creative, positive conflict right is one of the chairman's most difficult tasks. Too much argument and the organization becomes bogged down in politics; too little and the board develops a cosiness that rapidly becomes impervious to change signals.

Whether independent directors *do* add value is another question. For a whole variety of reasons we shall examine later, many companies do not gain any real value from their investment. Indeed, in some cases, they may have a negative value in that they hold up decision-making, or lend an image of respectability to a poorly performing executive management team.

On certain boards, where the chairman is very strong and the company largely his or her own creation—such as GEC, British Airways and Hanson—it is tempting to argue that board meetings are rather sedate and courteous affairs. There would not be the tough debate which preceded the decision at Abbey National to seek banking status. The former groups are 'good' companies but not always 'happy' and 'great' ones.

The independent directors at the first three need to be especially independent to be effective, but in practice in this kind of company they are often very close colleagues of the chairman.

The Arthur Andersen study compared the proportion of independent directors in a company with its financial performance. Its depressing conclusions suggest that most independent directors of public limited companies are ineffective and that the more independent directors packed on to a board, the worse the company's performance. Among companies in the upper quartile of performance, gearing was lower and dividend cover better, the fewer independent directors they had. The same picture emerged for earnings per share and pre-tax profit growth. Companies in this quartile, which have no independent directors, performed best of all, being three times as prudent in gearing as those with more than five independent directors. Companies with lots of independent directors performed slightly better in terms of return on capital employed, however.

At the other end of the financial performance scale, companies with multiple independent directors did better in most of the indicators.

These complex and apparently contradictory findings (a good example of the difference between data and information) can be explained in terms of what is expected of independent directors. In a company performing well, with a strong and effective management team, it is easy for the independent directors to become marginalized. Executive managers do not really *need* independent input—after all, they have most of the answers already, as evidenced by their success so far. The added value they seek from the board meetings becomes vague in concept, and therefore, more difficult to achieve. Moreover, in a highly successful company, the balance of power becomes even more heavily tipped towards the executives. Independent directors may be actively discouraged from getting too involved.

In the struggling company, on the other hand, it is a lot easier to see how the independent director can add value. Faced with severe, sometimes intractable problems, executive management is grateful for informed external advice and rather more inclined to listen. The impact of board decisions is also likely to be more immediate, encouraging a greater hands-on involvement by the independent directors.

To extract real value from independent directors, companies must provide a very clear definition of their role and what is expected of them. However, this frequently does not happen. According to one survey, 60 per cent of *The Times* 1000 companies appoint independent directors without defining their role. In another survey, by PA,[9] Sir Peter Laister, former chief executive of Thorn EMI, declared: 'No one has ever given me a piece of paper with my roles on it. I often wonder why I have been selected. Sometimes I find it is just because they think I can bring them business, which is the worst reason of all for appointing an independent director.'

Some useful guidance as to the primary duties of an independent director comes from The Working Group on Corporate Governance, in the United States.[10] Emphasizing that 'shareholders, particularly institutional shareholders who wish to be involved as owners, and directors have the common objective of promoting and supporting the ongoing prosperity of companies', the Working Group recommends:

1. The board of directors should evaluate the performance of the chief executive officer regularly against established goals and strategies.
2. This evaluation should be performed by 'outside' directors.
3. All outside directors should meet alone, at least once a year coordinated by a leader.
4. Directors should establish appropriate qualifications for board members and communicate those qualifications clearly to shareholders.
5. Outside directors should screen and recommend candidates based on qualifications established by the board.

The executive, who is approached to take up a post as independent director, should at the very least sit down before accepting to discuss with the chairman and other key directors, exactly how they see the role. Key questions might include:

- What strategic input would you expect an independent director to make into decisions on:
  - strategy in general
  - policy towards investors
  - technology strategy
  - marketing strategy
  - etc.
- To what extent are you willing to accept challenge to existing policies and strategies or are you just looking for endorsement of them?
- Do you want input at the early stages of strategy development or fine tuning at the later stages?
- Do the independent directors choose the chairman?
- How will my appointment affect the balance of the board in terms of independent director numbers and the mix of skills and personalities?
- To what extent are the independent directors expected to influence the board agenda?
- How, specifically, do you expect me to add value to the company?
- What vision do you have for the organization? Is it shared by the rest of the board?

If there are already other independent directors, you should ask them:

- What precisely is the input you make?
- To what extent do you feel (i) it is valued; (ii) it makes a difference?
- What frustrates you most about (i) this company; (ii) the board meetings?
- What excites you most?
- How open and free is discussion? Is criticism and detailed questioning welcomed?
- What, if any, areas of conflict are there between board members?
- Are there any 'no-go' areas for discussion?
- Who are the key personalities?
- What major decisions have you influenced?
- Do you feel as fully informed as you need to be?
- Is the board really a team?

THE BOARD MEETING

At one large UK company, the chairman made a deliberate policy of turning up 15 minutes late for board meetings. The reason? Experience had taught him that most of the independent directors would not have read the board papers properly beforehand; better to give them some reading time at the start of the meeting than to have them concentrating on the papers during discussions.

While this represents an extreme, it illustrates a major problem for many boards—basic lack of preparation, especially by independent directors. Indeed, lack of adequate preparation is a major cause of failure of independent director relationships. Sometimes this is the fault of the independent director; but equally, perhaps more often, it is a failure on the part of the company to keep the independent director informed in a timely, relevant and appropriate manner.

Key executives here means the company secretary as well. Indeed, almost invariably, the independent director is approached without talking to the company secretary who, after all, can inform the new independent director why certain items are included or not on previous board papers. By meeting the company secretary before the first board meeting at least the independent director will be familiar with two key faces.

In our survey of independent directors,[1] roughly 12 per cent of companies did not provide adequate information ahead of time.

Allister Wilson, of accountants Ernst & Young, writing in *The Times*,[11] expresses a common concern: 'The City agrees that the chief benefit of non-executive directors is their active participation as directors. Yet where a non-executive director's role is confined to examining vast piles of paper at a board meeting without the opportunity to raise freely issues of concern, then his or her ability to contribute to corporate debate is significantly constrained.'

John Mocatta, a company doctor who has been involved with over 100 boards, sometimes as chairman, chief executive or finance director, suggests the following guide to the financial information an independent director needs to perform the job effectively:

- Monthly management accounts comparing actual with budget for the most recent month and year to date and, if possible, showing the actual results for the same periods of the previous year.
- Detailed schedules showing debtors and creditors analysed on a monthly basis
- Detailed schedule of capital expenditure, comparing actual with budget for the most recent month and year to date and projecting forward for 12 months.
- Cash flow schedule comparing actual for most recent month with projected cash flow and extending projections for a period of 12 months.
- Schedule of anticipated forward orders and comments explaining why orders anticipated in the most recent month have not been received.

The scope of other information will depend to a very large extent on the board agenda. Typically the agenda should cover the following:

- *Record (minutes) of the previous meeting and actions arising.* A tedious formality if used as just a record, the minutes should provide a simple but effective method of checking what action has been taken to implement board policy.

    The need to preserve a legal record of the meeting means that the minutes are usually kept apart from the actions arising. Apart from checking for inaccuracies in reporting, the independent director should look for items that have not been implemented or have been implemented in a different way from that expected.
- *Performance review.* An analysis of performance against plans and budgets over the period. Some companies still confine this discussion to financial performance, but there is equal value in including measurements of performance against targets in areas such as:
    - R&D
    - quality improvement

- community investment
- upgrading of facilities and products
- introduction of new products
- employee development
- environmental performance

The independent director with a specialist functional expertise can be particularly helpful here.

There is a role for independent directors, too, in assessing performance in areas traditionally viewed as 'soft' and, therefore, hard to quantify. Often, the 'feel' of an organization, or the 'attitude of employees' is best evaluated by an outsider who is able to compare his or her own impressions over time. For a company attempting a major culture change, external feedback may be the only way to measure progress.

Other soft performance areas might include maintaining good relationships with City investors, enhancing the company's public image and boosting international standing in parts of the world where it has expansionist designs.

- *Presentations on major strategic/ competitive issues.* The independent director should not necessarily expect to have been given all the relevant papers on the theme ahead of time—particularly if an executive team has been asked to investigate an area and report back to the board. (Some or all of the executives may also be hearing the report for the first time.) However, the independent director should have had sufficient background briefing to be aware of the main issues and why the topic is on the agenda.

The purpose of such presentations should be for information rather than for decision-making. Strategic decisions do demand prior information and should be discussed as a tabled item on the agenda.

It is a valuable ploy to ask younger managers within the firm to make the occasional presentation to the main board. By so doing, the independent director can get a very good feel for some of the talent coming up through the organization.

- *Review of strategic threats and opportunities.* This is where the external perspective and experience of the independent director comes into its own. Some of the most effective independent directors respond to agenda items by bringing relevant documentation of their own—for example, publicly available reports or materials describing how their own company coped with a similar situation.

Acquisitions, mergers and the possibilities of takeover are common issues to arise at this point on the agenda. Here, the independent director will need to have prior knowledge both of the company's acquisition strategy in general, and of the other companies involved, in particular.

One immediate responsibility to arise out of this part of the independent director's role is to make sure that the information provided is understandable and sufficiently detailed for him or her to make informed comments and decisions. It is very difficult to establish the balance between being overwhelmed with paper and being under-informed, but experience is a good and rapid teacher. The company's willingness to comply with your information needs is a good indication of the role it wishes you to take and how seriously it regards that role.

In asking for broader, better presented information, the independent director often contributes significantly to the effectiveness of everyone at the meeting. Executive directors often have difficulty interpreting wadges of close columns of figures, even though they see them every month. It sometimes takes an outsider to stimulate a change to simplified presentation, with clear executive summaries.

Some companies now have regular pre-board meetings, at which they bring the independent directors up to speed on issues likely to arise at the board meeting proper. Our survey showed that 45 per cent of those companies which were seen by independent directors to provide adequate information had this sort of arrangement.

Comments former Legal & General chief executive Joe Palmer:

Two of the Boards on which I sit have a regular practice of informal meetings for non-executives in advance of formal Boards. In my view these are valuable if they are used essentially to bring non-executives 'up to speed', or are part of a chairman's procedure for taking soundings from the whole Board. Great care needs to be exercised by the chairman to make certain that these sessions, if they do not involve the whole Board at the same time, are not seen as a Board within a Board.

Clive Bastin, however, finds that 'properly minuted discussions with the chairman and/or chief executive in between meetings are a more appropriate format'.

However, Stephen Hayklan disagrees: 'I am against pre-Board meetings on the basis that if non-executives are so remote from the business that they need to be briefed, they are just wasting executives' time. The exception would be some very important and complex project that was coming up perhaps for the first time.'

Says Sir Nigel Mobbs: 'I have always found that holding short informal meetings to brief the non-executive directors has proved invaluable. This has avoided non-executive directors asking questions which delay the meeting and enables the chairman to brief non-executive directors on sensitive issues.'

'I always see non-executive directors privately before the board meeting', says Sir David Plaistow, chairman of Inchcape, 'so they can talk about more sensitive issues that can't be discussed at the meeting, and so they can form a team approach. There should always be a luncheon after the board meeting, too, so that the non-executives have a chance to get to know the executives better.'

In the absence of such formal briefings, the independent director can and should still insist on having the information he or she needs to carry out the role. A common practice among valued independent directors is to telephone or fax a series of requests for further information ahead of the meeting. At the very least, this means that executives will be able to answer questions at the meeting, if not before.

Once again, Sir Lewis Robertson provides a useful summation:

It is important to the non-executive directors above all that the Board's discussions should be well-structured. An ordered agenda, sufficient but not overkill of detail in Board papers, adequate time to prepare, good timing and pacing of meetings, wise use of advisors and good chairmanship in the basic, discussion-handling sense, all these things are important in enabling the external directors to deliver the contribution they can bring, and these things the chairman is responsible for ensuring.

It is a matter of balancing the need for information against the practical constraints that mean executives will always be better informed.

In practice, the amount and type of information available is a strong indication of how the executives and the chairman in particular regard the board. After all, legally, the independent director is entitled to any information about the company that is available to the executive directors. In general, the more open the company is in providing information to its independent directors, the more it is likely to value their input and the clearer they are likely to be about why they are there.

However, the control of information flow is very much in the hands of the executives and it is relatively easy to conceal information the independent directors might not like. Says Sir Antony Pilkington: 'You can give [independent directors] as little or as much as you want depending on the sort of board papers presented to them and the time you give them to consider them.' In several cases where companies have come into conflict with the law, the executives were able to turn round to the non-executive directors and say: 'But you never asked for that information!' It is very difficult to ask questions about problems you do not know exist!

The Merton Associates study of 1991[6] found that only 30 per cent of independent directors were satisfied with the adequacy and accuracy of the briefings they received. Just under 60 per cent felt their contribution was being severely compromised by the poor quality of briefings given by the chairman or chief executive. Our own survey[1] suggests that 91 per cent of independent directors feel they have enough information to make informed decisions at board meetings. (This does not directly contradict the Merton results—

dissatisfaction with information on wider issues is likely to be higher.) As an observation unsupported by statistical evidence, the authors suggest that public limited companies (with major exceptions such as the Maxwell companies) are more likely to provide adequate *boardroom* information than family companies, but when it comes to operational information, the opposite may often be true (because the executives in the family company are often much better informed themselves in these areas).

The independent directors we interviewed tended to agree in general that the responsibility for ensuring information is provided rests in practical terms on the non-executives themselves. Says Dr Brian Smith:

Independent directors should insist on having the company's operating data regularly and on time. Independent directors should be sure that the information is reliable by talking to the auditors. These two elements form the paper checks.

Independent directors should go out and talk to people in the company. The paper checks are no guarantee that things are as they should be. You should visit sites and let people— management and employees—know that you are accessible and approachable. They must know that you are not just another part of the 'establishment'. That allows you to keep an ear to the ground for anything that's amiss. The independent director role goes beyond the performance of the company. You need to know if the truth is being suppressed, which is a question of culture. The data you receive on paper tells you about today only. As an independent director your job is to be concerned about what will happen in the future as well. If you are to know both where the company is and where it is going, you must monitor the culture.

When I visit sites I don't go to see the management. The last time I visited Heathrow as part of my job at BAA, for instance, I went to see the people who work on the apron. The time before I talked to the people in security. However, there is another important point here. If, based on those visits, I think action is required I tell someone. I do not take the action myself. I am not in an executive role so it is not my job. If I were to try to take action myself I would be transgressing.

At BAA, we encourage our new independent directors to spend some time walking around and talking to people. It is not possible to put a face to a company from pieces of paper. You need to get the feel and the smell of the business which comes from mixing with the people on the ground.

Pat Rich, chairman and chief executive of BOC, and an independent director of an international packaging group puts it this way: 'It is a director's prerogative to ask for no surprises. The withholding of information is grounds for an attack on the management and for resignation if you cannot reach a satisfactory solution. A good chief executive should present the non-executive directors with a model, or schedule, which sets out the timing of the information they need.'

Having dutifully prepared, the independent director should aim to maximize his or her contribution to value creation at the board meeting itself. At its simplest, this boils down to *when* to comment and *how* to comment.

When to comment

As equals to all the other directors, independent directors should feel free to comment whenever they have something useful to say. Certainly they should ask questions to clarify their own understanding. Never be frightened to appear, naïve, to keep asking 'why'. It is like taking a child to the zoo—the more naïve the questions the more both adult and child learn.

Equally, independent directors should comment when they have useful insights to offer, or concerns to raise. In particular, they should be able to adopt the perspective of stakeholders in the business and explore issues on their behalf. As Archie Norman, chief executive of ASDA and independent director of Geest plc expresses it: 'The purpose of non-executive directors is not least to solidify the relationship between that company and the shareholders and to make sure that the shareholders' views are properly expressed and represented on the Board.'

In a small number of companies, the independent directors have a special mandate from shareholders. For example, National Freight Consortium, one of the early 'privatizations', has a director elected by and on behalf of the small share-holders, many of whom will be employees.

In practice, most issues that arise at board meetings should provide an opportunity for the independent director to comment or at least ask questions. Any item that does not, probably should not be on the agenda at all. On the other hand, the independent director is not there to offer opinions for the sake of it. There are often issues arising that are not appropriate for discussion at the meeting, but which should be subsequently raised with individual directors. A caution-ary tale is told of a well-known personality appointed to the board of a major privatized company. After a couple of board meetings, he was counselled by a colleague to say less and listen more.

It is difficult to say which is worse: the independent direc-tor who has little to say on anything, or the person who cannot prevent himself or herself from offering an opinion on everything. The bigger the board and the more independent directors, the worse either extreme becomes. The non-contributor becomes less obvious, while several windbags can make board meetings drag on forever.

Comments one independent director: 'Whilst the value of an independent director's insight into a new dimension for the Board is important he should use this skill carefully and by reference to other outsiders. There is nothing worse than an independent director know-it-all!'

Adds another independent director: 'There is a tendency for independent directors to discuss at considerable length the colour of the loo doors and it is very important for them to realise the value and cost of the Board's time. People with a propensity for the nitty-gritty don't necessarily make the best independent directors.'

A number of independent directors express concern that the Cadbury proposals[12] would oblige them to become too involved in detail, undermining their ability to retain a strate-gic focus. Jim Beveridge, finance director of MEPC and independent director of Cardiff Bay Development Corpor-ation, for example, urges strongly that 'we should use the independent director's time effectively and not bog them down in detail'.

A useful guideline for deciding when to speak up might be:

- Is what I have to say really relevant to the issue?
- Is it simply repeating a point made by someone else, or can I add weight to that view with further information?
- Will it help us reach the correct decision?
- What precisely am I trying to achieve? Is this the right forum for doing so?
- Is it better to come from me or an executive director?

This last issue, which we could call clarity of purpose, is very dependent on situation. Essentially, the director intervenes for one of the following reasons:

- To gain personal understanding of the issue.
- To clarify the options for everyone around the table.
- To propose alternative ways of looking at an issue (innovative, unconventional thinking can be a great asset to the board).
- To propose a specific course of action.
- To support or oppose a course of action proposed by someone else.

If the chairman is weak, it may also be legitimate to intervene to bring discussions back to the point. However, if this continues to be the case, it must raise questions about the effectiveness of the top team: long rambling discussions are often a sign of a company with weak leadership and poor sense of purpose generally. A good reason for appointing an independent chairman—particularly in entrepreneurial companies—is to being discipline and focus to board meetings.

The independent director should also be prepared to introduce topics to the agenda of his or her own volition. In some cases, these may be issues discovered through discussions with employees; in others, a significant issue of relevance may have arisen in the company where he or she is an executive. The independent director can introduce the latter with the added benefit of being able to summarize the thinking and discussion that has already taken place in his or her company—saving excessive debate at the host board.

From time to time, the independent director may be approached by executive directors, who wish to bring up a topic for discussion, but for various reasons of internal politics, feel unable to do so themselves. Once again, this is a valuable service the independent director can provide, but care should be taken to ensure that he or she is not being used to help promote a hobby-horse of the executive concerned.

Sir Anthony Gill, chairman and chief executive of Lucas plc, relates a fairly typical example.

> The executives on one Board where I am a non-executive director were talking about an ambitious programme of change. But they had not put in place the structures to ensure that the vast number of projects they were embarking on could be inter-related and prevented from competing for the same resources. Because my company uses programme management approaches all the time, I was able to ask how they were going to deal with these issues. They had to ask me what I meant and I explained what was needed. If I hadn't been there, no-one would have asked the essential questions.

How to comment

The balance between harmony and rancour can sometimes be a fine one. A major justification for appointing independent directors is that they should present a different view from people working full-time in the company. Allowed to express their views, they will inevitably (if they have any degree of competence) stimulate debate.

Maintaining that debate on an even keel, ensuring it is productive rather than destructive, is the job of the chairman. Says Sir Lewis Robertson: 'Personal chemistry is crucial but indefinable. It is a key skill to be able to disagree, but agreeably; to differ, without splitting apart and to criticise, but constructively. It is the chairman's duty to think always of personal chemistry and to keep an unobtrusive but always open eye on relationships.'

Lucas's Gill reinforces the point: 'An open, direct but polite style works best—one where differences get aired in a way that stops short of conflict. But it would be a mistake to organise the Board to avoid conflict—then you'd never have genuine challenge.'

Adds Gordon Owen: 'As an independent director start by saying "have you thought of the following?" This almost sums up the role. Don't ask "why didn't you do that?" which, alas, is more common and is really an executive director's question, because quite often they haven't.'

The ability to speak plainly and forcefully without giving offence is indeed a skill and is perhaps one of the most important qualities to look for in an effective independent director. It can be very easy for an individual independent director or a small group to become cast in the role of guer-rillas—a solid opposition group determined to question any-thing and everything the executives do. To a certain extent, when such circumstances develop, they usually do so at least in part because the executive team is not mature enough to welcome constructive criticism; but it may equally be that the independent director forgets that he or she is there to assist the executives in thinking issues through, rather than to act as Grand Inquisitor or to do their jobs for them.

Consultant Kep Simpson illustrates how sensitively an independent director may have to behave:

> I serve as one of three independent directors on a board of an entrepreneur-owned company. We sat down with the managing director, who was the major shareholder, over beer and sand-wiches one evening and got him to see that the future develop-ment of the business (and therefore his own fortune) would fare better with a different style of top management. Since we couldn't fill the bill any other way, we concluded that the only thing to do was to sell the company to another, where the right management was available. The merchant bank agreed.
>
> We were only able to come to this agreement because the independent directors had a strong rapport with the managing director. The independent director has to be cordial and abso-lutely straight. It's one of the functions of a good friend to be able to say unpalatable things in a way the recipient will see as helpful.
>
> It also illustrates the need for the independent director to be fully independent of the company, so he can give genuinely impartial advice. After all, we were selling ourselves out of a job in this case.

Clive Bastin adds to the political discussion:

> A successful independent director must always retain the respect of his colleagues. That respect is shown both in and outside of the boardroom and in the willingness of the executive directors to use the advice of the independent directors at all times outside of meetings where such advice can add value. A successful independent director inevitably walks the tightrope between on the one side speaking up on all issues where he feels in disagreement with his colleagues, thereby being accused of not being a member of a team, and on the other side so agreeing with his colleagues that he does not bring an independent view or indeed contrary view to challenge management. One thing is certain, an independent director soon recognises whether he is leaning too far either side of the tightrope!

The need for collective goodwill, no matter how fierce the debate, is paramount; but what of those situations, where the independent director is convinced the company is heading in the wrong direction or, worse still, that the executive team is acting unethically or illegally? One option is to resign, although this may not be very effective in protecting the independent director's public reputation later. Most independent directors would argue that they have responsibility towards the shareholders to force issues out into the open, first at the board meeting, where alternative views can be expressed, then, if necessary more publicly by, for example, discussing the matter with the Stock Exchange.

Sir Lewis Robertson asks:

> How do non-executive directors without in any way forming a permanent, overt opposition, ensure that the basics of management and of corporate governance are observed, and that the wrong happenings that have lately been so much in the public eye, sometimes disgraceful, sometimes dishonest, sometimes just plain stupid, do not recur, but are nipped in the bud and prevented?

The answer, in many cases, is that they do not. Marketeer Jerry Shively became one of two non-executive directors of dry-cleaning company Sketchley in 1987. Here is an abbreviated version of his story, as told to *The Financial Times*:[13]

My first impression was positive. A relatively new and aggressive management team was anxious to use acquisition as a tool of company growth, while maintaining enough profit to keep dividends high (and presumably the share price up).

In reality, the executives were on an acquisitions 'high' and only listened with half an ear to the independent directors' warnings about rushing headlong into opportunities.

Managers and directors have basically three things with which to work: information, instinct and experience.' Information seemed to be sufficient—reports were well-presented at monthly board meetings, by the directors responsible. But, admits Shively, he should have given greater weight to his instincts.

The first sign that anything was wrong came about when Sketchely bought a vending company to strengthen its existing business in the area. The independent directors questioned accounting procedures and inventory values and were told that 'enough allowances had been made'. It ultimately transpired that the inventory figure was inflated by £1 million, as a result of failure to write down the value of returned equipment.

Other warning signs were a curt reaction from the chairman to 'a naive but well-intentioned question'—a growing sense that the independent directors were a tolerated imposition; the way in which the executives dismissed any discussion of their three year contracts; and the fact that a key report on the company's future, by a management consultancy firm, was made to the executives only, rather than to the Board as a whole.

Not long after, the chairman called an emergency Board meeting to discuss a dramatic profits collapse, as a result of problems with the vending acquisition. Shively and his colleague John Gillum then found themselves presiding over the gradual replacement of the whole top management team (including, ultimately, themselves).

'Should we non-executives have been more persistent in challenging the company's managers?' asks Shively, answering his own question with 'Yes ... having asked and received answers, we failed to press our inquiries.'

Of course, an independent director should not approach every board meeting with the view that the executive directors are consciously or unconsciously trying to hide important data. That would hardly be conducive to harmonious working relationships. On the other hand, one of the main reasons so many independent directors are ineffective is that they do not ask the penetrating questions they should and, through pressures of time or not wanting to make waves, are deterred at the first barrier from pursuing potential areas of concern.

Says Sir David Plaistow, chairman of Inchcape:

> The quality of preparation for board meetings is very important. So is a free and frank exchange. I've been on boards where there is such a driving chairman that there is no discussion. I've quit or taken other action where it has been necessary. With Saunders at Guinness, for example, it was quite demanding from November 1986 until we got Tennant in place. We did most of the work in the evenings with lawyers.
>
> The final trigger came when a solicitor rang me up and said: 'My partner concerned with the Guinness audit tells me you've been fully briefed about a series of unusual payments.' I hadn't and we had to face up to the situation.
>
> At Guinness there were five of us; new outside directors acting in unison. On another board I had to threaten the chairman that unless he found more effective non-executive directors, I'd quit. He got them.

The key to handling these situations is for the independent director to recognize that he or she has a *right* to the information and to explain why he or she needs to exercise that right. To retain long-term credibility with investors a company not only has to be well managed, it has to be seen to be well managed. If the independent director cannot obtain a straight answer at board level, he or she should use contacts lower down in the organization to explore their understanding of the issues.

It is also important to use instinct and experience to warn of impending problems. Shively's mentor, Sam Johnson of the eponymous Johnson's Wax told him: 'The primary job of the non-executive director is to avoid disaster'—and that means keeping an eye open for the obvious signs of trouble. Sir Lewis Robertson, as always, has a relevant comment: 'Watch for a number of signs and symptoms: a management that is beginning to be left behind by the company's growth; a lack of product development; a failure of marketing flair; bad personnel relations ... every company will encounter difficulties, but when difficulties persist and do not seem to be firmly addressed, management change and improvement is needed.'

A recent study by one of the authors[14] into business failure found seven common sets of attitude among the executive teams:

- *Attitudes towards controls*—not just financial, but also technical and managerial.
- *Attitudes towards the business vision*—how well it is shared and endorsed by other people; how well-founded it proves.
- *Attitudes towards the team*—is there truly a team at the top, or is there a dictator and yes-men? In many cases of failure, there is a small inner circle of people who, while nominally top managers, are not genuinely committed and involved in key decisions.
- *Attitudes towards customers*—do the executives really understand customer motivations?
- *Attitudes towards investors*—are they seen as business partners or a damned nuisance?
- *Attitudes towards learning*—does top management see itself as continually learning, or do they know it all already?
- *Attitudes towards winning and losing*—are the executives really in business to succeed, or to have a comfortable life?

In addressing such issues at board level, the independent director needs first to gain agreement that they are relevant matters for the board to consider. That may be the hardest part of all, particularly with an executive team who do not want to face up to reality, or a board which is unclear about the difference between strategy and tactics. This is where previous experience can be valuable, allowing the independent director to point out the problems other companies have faced from not addressing the issue.

Having gained agreement to discuss the matter, even if reluctantly, the independent director should marshall support before the board meeting, either from fellow independent directors, or through reports from senior managers or consultants. The latter course assumes that the independent director is permitted by the company to use resources in this way—if he or she is not, then the company is effectively saying it does not value the independent director's view.

Any presentation the independent director makes should be of at least the same professional standard as that made by the executives.

One independent director describes some of the political issues involved:

> No independent director should be frightened of speaking up on a major issue even if his colleagues are not of the same mind. However, his views will carry more weight if he has the support of any fellow independent directors. Politics play a part in all board meetings and if the chairman or chief executive are to be persuaded to go a different direction from that recommended then inevitably the independent directors need the support of other executive directors. Constant disagreements between independent directors and the executive directors lead to extremely poor meetings and relationships—even accusations that the independent directors are not behaving in the best interests of shareholders.

HOW INDEPENDENT DIRECTORS COULD CONTRIBUTE MORE AT BOARD MEETINGS

- *They are inadequately informed, so have no knowledge, on which to base observations.* In Thorn EMI's annual report,[15] Sir Peter Walters, the independent deputy chairman, was at great pains to emphasize that this was not the case for him and his colleagues. In a separate section, Corporate Governance, he writes:

> To contribute effectively to the decision-making process in Thorn EMI, the non-executive directors and I need information about the company to be displayed openly. We need frank and critical debate. Only in this way can confidence in the integrity and ability of the executive management develop. I can assure shareholders that we enjoy both total access to the facts and vigorous uninhibited discussion with the executive directors whom, you may notice, we outnumber.

As we mentioned earlier, companies which want to ensure their independent directors are well informed, often have pre-board meetings. Kep Simpson again:

> At a family company, where I am an independent director, we have a dinner once a quarter before the Board meeting. It may go on till 2 or 3 am. By the time we get to sleep we have rehearsed all the key issues. Because there is no formality over the dinner, you hear what people think rather than what they want minuted. We find Board issues are treated in a much better way and that we don't waste time on trivia.

- *They are too close to the executive chairman or chief executive and are therefore reluctant to challenge him or her openly* (a real friend would be sure to do so, either at the meeting or subsequently).
- *They are scared of losing the job, so do not wish to offend.*
- *They are insufficiently interested.* This is probably only one of many independent directorships they hold, so they lack the deep fascination with the business that characterizes so many effective independent directors.
- *The board is badly constructed or chaired.* For example, it may simply have too many independent directors to allow for reasonable, focused debate.
- *They do not have a good relationship with the chairman.* The 1991 survey of non-executive directors by Merton Associates[6] found that 'discord between chairmen and independent directors is rife' and that nearly three out of five felt the chairman did not heed objective advice.
- *The board meets so infrequently that they never have an opportunity to get to know the company.*
- *They are not as independent as they seem.* A 1992 survey by Pensions Investment Research Consultants, looking at 52 FTSE companies, found 18 non-executive directors 'who could not be classified as fully independent under Institutional Shareholders' Committee guidelines. They include Sir Peter Walters, a non-executive director of SmithKline Beecham, who is also the chairman of its lead banker, Midland Bank and Neil Shaw, a non-executive director of United Biscuits and also chairman of Tate & Lyle, one of UB's big suppliers.'(*The Times*, 5 May 1992)[16]

OUTSIDE THE BOARDROOM

The degree to which the independent director becomes involved with the company outside the board meetings, will depend on many factors, not least the time available (people with a portfolio of independent director positions are unlikely to have time to become more than superficially involved in any of them) and how willing the executives are to share power.

John Allan, executive main board director at BET comments: 'It is possible to hold several non-executive positions and make a useful contribution at Board meetings. However, once you get beyond a certain point, I believe it is difficult to find the time to add value beyond that Boardroom contribution.' On the other hand, it is clear that the greater the independent director's involvement, the greater his or her potential influence.

John Hestlegrave has worked on over a dozen boards as a non-executive director. In this capacity, as well as working as a consultant, he has taken a number of companies on what he describes as 'away-from-it-all strategic think-tanks'. He sees the independent director's key role as being to 'help the other people on the Board to change their mindsets. Executives often get into a rut in the way they think and work, especially if they are responsible for a specific function. The non-executives can get them to think as a Board rather than a collection of vying and competing individuals.' Hestlegrave points out that, particularly in times of recession, day-to-day concerns can become predominant, resulting in a lack of clarity of goals. In companies which have a non-executive chairman this insistence on working as a team and seeing with helicopter vision can be his or her job. Other companies must rely on the non-executives as a group. Hestlegrave says that, in his experience, non-executives are often excluded from these 'think-tank' meetings—yet often it is exactly at these meetings where they can contribute most and get the most out of the opportunity to get to know the other members of the board better and develop ways of working with them.

The most common additional responsibility is membership of sub-committees of the board, in particular the executive remuneration/compensation committee, the audit committee and the shareholders' committee. Other possible committees might be the ethics policy committee, or, in a small company, the marketing committee.

The compensation committee, suggests a raft of observers, should normally have a majority of independent directors. Indeed PRO NED argues it should be composed entirely of independent directors, or at least of people who will not benefit from its decisions.

The Cadbury Committee's Report on Corporate Governance[12] echoes the PRO NED view, recommending that

> Boards should appoint remuneration committees, consisting wholly or mainly of non-executive directors and chaired by a non-executive director, to recommend to the Board the remuneration of the executive directors in all its forms, drawing on outside advice as necessary. Executive directors should play no part in decisions on their own remuneration. Membership of the remuneration committee should appear in the Directors' Report and its chairman should be responsible for answering questions on remuneration principles and practice at the Annual General Meeting.

One of the major problems of compensation committees is that the independent directors may be reluctant to oppose over-generous pay, bonus and profit-share arrangements for the executives. The cynical might observe that the great and good have half an eye on what might happen in their own companies' compensation committees and it is difficult to discount this entirely as a motivation. Of greater influence, we suspect, however, is simple reluctance to rock the boat.

A 1991 report for the Chartered Institute of Management Accountants (CIMA)[17] supports this view. Professor Andrew Likierman, of London Business School, who was one of the authors of the report, explains: 'If the non-executive directors are simply the golfing pals of the chairman, there is no point in these committees.' The fact that independent directors are appointed by the board and only ratified as rubber stamped by shareholders acts to reinforce the cosiness of the relationship.

Arthur Andersen's Corporate Register suggests that

although non-executive directors are supposed to act as an arbiter of pay levels ... 'they appear singularly to fail to fulfil their obligations. However the company is performing, it seems to be a golden rule that the more non-executives on the Board, the higher the salaries for the highest paid directors.'

In practice, remuneration committees can vary from rubber stamps to stormy affairs. The committee can have bite when the chairman wants to grant himself an insensitive increase. There have been too many examples of executive greed packaged to disguise the fact and put before a remuneration committee. Unfortunately, often the independent directors are of a poor quality and prove no check and balance. Sometimes the mere packing of a remuneration committee with truly effective independent directors prevents the potential remuneration embarrassment in the first place. To be effective, the independent director must also avoid becoming part of the company's pay structure. It is hard to be both judge and jury.

Recently, an independent director candidate asked the interview panel, composed of existing independent directors, what the salary would be. When told £15,000, he said it was not enough. If offered £20,000 he would join and it would help the existing independent directors raise their own salaries. And that is what happened. Some of these independent directors were also on the company's remuneration committee!

In another case, a group of non-executive directors were asked to develop a fair remunerations policy which would prevent settlements out of proportion to performance. They came up with such a weak plan that the chairman threw them out of his office, telling them to go away and come up with something better.

Another explanation might lie in the results of a PRO NED survey in 1990,[18] which explored just what happens in remuneration committees. The survey found that in only 31 per cent of cases was an independent director the chairman of the remuneration committee; in 62 per cent it was the chairman of the board and in 5 per cent the chief executive. The survey also concluded that the committee members often had inadequate data about salary and compensation trends; that the consultants called in to advise on such issues were often less independent than they might seem; and that independent directors were unjustifiably complacent about how well they handled the task of balancing the interests of top management and shareholders in setting top pay levels. 'There are probably few other areas', said the report, 'where the chairman or chief executives would award themselves such high marks for the decisions they have taken. This alone suggests that the process of decision-making by remuneration committees requires re-appraisal. Is it truly objective and free from undue pressure?'

The CIMA report[17] explains that part of the problem may be inadequate information available to independent members of the remuneration committee. While CIMA found no evidence to support assertions that executives overstate their companies' performance to boost performance-related pay, it did conclude that the accounting links between business performance and remuneration systems were inadequate. It also concluded that the guidelines, under which remuneration committees operate, were too vague to allow sufficiently well-considered decisions. These issues are increasingly pre-occupying independent directors—not least, because the solutions are not always obvious.

What *should* happen in remuneration committees is that the independent directors should take responsibility for acquiring the information about good practice and pay standards, which they need to reach independent decisions. They should not simply accept data provided by the company, nor advice from consultants who are employed by the company in some other activity.

PRO NED found in a survey[18] that, while 69 per cent of quoted companies had remuneration committees, one-third of these committees included executive directors. PRO NED recommends remuneration committees should be 100 per cent non-executives. In this context, genuine independence is probably helped if the majority of independent directors on the committee are not main board directors of other large companies, but drawn from a wider spectrum of society.

The primary responsibility of the independent director is to the shareholders rather than to the executives. A certain level of incentive is proper and necessary to motivate exceptional financial performance; but the line between effective incentives and excessive generosity can be a fine one. As in so many management decisions, the acid test may often be: what would the informed man in the street regard as fair and reasonable?

The secrecy that accompanies the deliberations of compensation committees' deliberations often makes matters worse.

Says CIMA: 'In contrast to the often higher level of disclosure in the United States, the public in the UK usually has no idea upon what performance criteria managers are being judged.'

As management writer Clare Hogg points out:

Most experts are agreed that the best way to deal with senior executive pay is to be completely open and above board about how it is calculated and agreed. There should be 'glasnost' in its determination. Even if the awards are realistic, responsible and competitive, if the methodology behind them is not disclosed companies are leaving themselves open to unnecessary criticism.

It is not just the methodology which must be seen to be scrupulously fair.

Compensation levels should be set by a snowy-white group of individuals. There are limits to the independence of many non-executive directors, often they are appointed by managers and not shareholders. Often they are on each other's boards. Remuneration committees should be composed of individuals with no axe to grind'.

PRO NED has developed a set of guidelines to help independent directors ensure the remuneration process is fair, that it is fully discussed and, therefore, able to be defended.

The independent directors should insist that directors' salaries and bonuses are published at the time they are granted, rather than allow the announcement to be delayed to the AGM and explain how they were arrived at. Paradoxically, this ought to work to the executives' advantage, because the remuneration can be related in stakeholders' minds directly to the period it covers, rather than to the circumstances some months later, when the company's fortunes may have taken a turn for the worse. A number of independent directors have commented that, while they have been unable to persuade executives to moderate large salary increases, they have been able to gain agreement on how and when to communicate what has been decided.

Sir Peter Walters, again in the Thorn EMI annual report:

> I also chair the compensation committee, of which the chairman is the only executive member. We settle the remuneration and other terms of employment of the executive directors and— without his presence—of the chairman. We consider senior executive succession plans and related issues. The grant of options under the Executive Share Option Scheme is decided by a committee consisting only of non-executive directors under my chairmanship.

The audit committee demands at least a moderate understanding of corporate finance and the doggedness to pursue signs of poor control. However, the study by Merton Associates[6] found 'strong evidence... about a lack of awareness by non-executive directors over the need to sustain and safeguard a corporate image for "economical housekeeping"'.

Sir Lewis Robertson says:

> The non-executive directors should ensure that the company's finances are balanced, its relations with its lenders carefully tended and its borrowings held in careful balance with its capacity to service and cover them. It is not difficult for management to be carried away in boom times by over-easy access to finance; the non-executive directors should watch this dimension.

Audit committees (which in the United States must have a majority of independent directors) in quoted companies have a number of specific, formal roles, including the following:

- Appointing external auditors, and ensuring they are independent, reputable and capable; agreeing the audit fee.
- To review the interim and final results of the company with the external auditors.

- To arbitrate between executive management and the auditors if there is disagreement over the conduct or content of financial reporting.
- To ensure the company operates efficient systems of financial management and reporting, internally as well as externally.
- To receive regular reports from the chief internal auditor.

In addition, the audit committee may ask the auditors to carry out other investigations, to recommend improvements in financial management systems, and so on. The members must also be prepared to respond to alarm calls by the auditors— for example, if the executive management ignores recommendations by internal or external auditors. In short, they must do everything they can to maintain the financial probity and integrity of the company.

Shareholder committees are often established where there is shareholder dissatisfaction, which in turn is often a result of autocratic chairmanship or where a company is performing badly.

Pension funds are normally administered by trustees, who may include directors. It may often be appropriate for an independent director to act as one of the trustees, not least from the point of view of reassuring employees that a watchdog is present. (It is also helpful for the independent director to be aware of his or her own pension arrangements through the company.)

John Hackman, former chairman of New England Properties plc, is also an expert on pension funds and the role of the independent director. He explains:

> The company often takes major policy decisions in respect of pensions. Even if there is an independent director present, his role is often very marginal—yet there are major *policy* decisions involved, rather than just technical pension points. The success of the company is directly related to that of its pension fund as the fund's performance determines the requirement for future contributions from the company. In the extreme case, for example, if the company went bust and the pension fund was invested in the parent company then the pension fund could go down as well. There are limits on the amount that can be invested in this way, but the law still offers inadequate cover.

There are also major areas where the independent director can play a part in discussing what the company should do with any pension surplus. Decisions such as whether to provide benefit enhancement through early retirement or other additions to benefits or whether to return the surplus to the company are policy decisions not detailed pension points. It is not for the independent director to interfere in management pay below Director level but benefits for all employees involve a major company policy decision.

Hackman recommends that all large companies, at the very least, should have independent director trustees on their pension funds.

An interesting and revealing description of the involvement of independent directors in board committees is provided by Figure 4.2. In the 1991 annual report of Grand Metropolitan, deputy chairman Dick Giordano addressed an open letter to shareholders[19] (see pp. 136–7).

Another major area of activity outside the boardroom is counselling of either the chief executive or other executives.

According to Sir Antony Pilkington, giving evidence to The Trade and Industry Committee of the House of Commons in 1991:[20]

> The relationship is basically between the chairman and his non-executive directors. He looks upon them as a sounding board and a critical part of the management and direction of his company. For instance, I meet my non-executive directors at least twice a year, alone, to enable them to make comments directly to me which they might find difficult to make in a full Board meeting.

Other tasks include that of general ambassador, representing the company at public events, to parliamentary committees or to the investment community. However, it is important that the independent director should not do the chairman's job for him.

A good deal of time may also be spent on getting to know people at other levels in the organization, and on helping them deal with specific problems and opportunities. The independent director may, for example, be able to contribute valuable advice on the following:

- *The viability of new ideas.* Although the managers may have access to a wide variety of advice, both internal and external, an independent view from an outsider with a different set of experiences can provide useful insights into what will or will not work.
- *Pushing through change.* The independent director cannot be a change driver *per se*—major change programmes have to be led by the executive team. He or she can, however, provide valuable support, talking through tactics to implement change and putting the weight of his or her experience behind decisions.

Sir Lewis Robertson again:

The non-executive cannot properly function as a company doctor. He can play a really vital role in preventive medicine, and he or she can serve as a key player in bringing in the remedial doctor when required; but the full remedial job, the gutsy, risky stuff at the wilder shores of corporate life, does not seem to be accessible to a director who not only does not hold final executive power, but has to work alongside someone who does ... Non-executive directors ... cannot be the performers of change but the facilitators of it.

In making these contributions it is helpful—some would say essential—for the independent director to have his or her own sources of advice, and if possible a working base outside the company, to avoid becoming too reliant on the company's own resources.

When independent directors fail to contribute outside the boardroom, the cause is most often lack of time. But other factors—unwillingness by the executives to involve them, lack of appropriate expertise, or unwillingness by the independent directors to take responsibility—are also common.

A good measure of the commitment on both sides to genuine involvement is whether the independent directors and executives spend quality time together outside the boardroom. For example, all the independent directors at Johnson Matthey join top management for the company's annual strategy conference, which lasts approximately two days. The non-executives make a major contribution to this

From Richard V Giordano KBE (USA)

Dear Shareholder,

In accordance with UK law and custom the entire Board of Directors is accountable to the shareholders and other stakeholders for the stewardship of the company's assets and activities. However, the non-executive directors do have a special role in Corporate Governance. Their independence is particularly valuable in audit and remuneration matters, and you will see below that the two Board Committees dealing with these subjects are staffed and chaired solely by non-executives.

The non-executive directors also have a significant role in ensuring that the company's business and financial strategies, and the opportunities and risks associated with those strategies, are fully vetted in the Boardroom. They also have a major role to play in planning the succession of top management, including that of the Chairman and Chief Executive.

Since the non-executive directors all carry major responsibilities outside GrandMet, I see it as my task as Deputy Chairman to provide leadership and focus in the discharge of those responsibilities which are unique to their independent, non-executive role.

In the normal course of business the whole Board operates as a team under the chairmanship of Sir Allen Sheppard. We meet at least eight times a year including a two day strategy conference. Effective management of a large and active group, however, requires that many duties and activities be delegated to Board Committees, and GrandMet now has seven of these:

Appraisal and Remuneration: Consisting of the four non-executive directors only, chaired by myself, this Committee performs the task of measuring the performance of the executive directors and certain other key executives as a prelude to determining their annual remuneration, bonus awards and awards of long term incentives. Performance is measured against the achievement of personal objectives and profit and cash targets and a substantial part of their total remuneration depends on the growth in the value of GrandMet's share price over the medium and long term. This Committee is also the forum within which top management succession is discussed for recommendations to the full Board.

Audit: This also consists only of the four non-executive directors, chaired by David Simon. This Committee ensures that accounting and financial policies and controls are in place and that internal and external auditing processes are properly coordinated and work effectively. This ensures, for example, that it is reasonable for full reliance to be placed on the integrity and consistency of the figures in this Annual Report.

Chairman's Committee: Consisting of the five executive directors and the executives responsible for group strategy and corporate affairs, this Committee meets monthly under Sir Allen Sheppard's chairmanship to review and determine all policy matters not specifically reserved to the Board or another Board Committee.

Community Affairs: Chaired by David Tagg, this Committee comprises the members of the Chairman's Committee and meets twice a year to agree the strategic plans and operating budgets for charitable and community activities throughout the group.

Group Operations: This Committee discusses policy and operational issues which affect the group as a whole. It meets four times a year with Sir Allen Sheppard as Chairman. Its membership consists of the members of the Chairman's Committee, the Group Legal Director and Company Secretary and five senior general managers.

Management Development: Chaired by Ian Martin, this Committee meets twice a year to consider overall development and succession issues and to review specific development plans for the top 250 executives in the group. Membership consists of the Chairman's Committee and myself.

Nomination: This Committee consists of Sir Allen Sheppard and the two longest serving non-executive directors, Sir John Harvey-Jones and myself. It meets as appropriate to consider possible changes to Board or Board Committee membership and to make recommendations to the full Board.

The non-executives are represented on four of the seven Board Committees. The minutes of **all** Committee Meetings, internal studies on strategy and business development, as well as detailed monthly reports about current issues and financial performance, are circulated to **all** Board Members. I am confident that we are kept well informed. Board discussions are lively and uninhibited, and the experience and advice of the non-executive directors are sought and, even when unpalatable, welcomed.

All in all I believe that we, the non-executives, are making our contribution to the continued success of GrandMet.

Richard V. Giardano

Figure 4.2 An open letter from the deputy chairman of Grand Metropolitan to its shareholders.

meeting which undoubtedly also helps them in their role as directors of the company.

SUMMARY

The competencies of an independent director are different from those of both executive directors and managers. To be truly effective, an independent director must recognize those differences and seize opportunities to develop the relative skills. While very little training in independent direction is yet available, companies can help to enhance the capability of the directors as a team. Only by having clearly defined roles and learning opportunities can the company make a viable assessment of the performance of individual independent directors.

REFERENCES

1. Making the most of Non-Executive Directors—a survey by Hanson Green and The ITEM Group plc, 1992.
2. Enhancing Boardroom Effectiveness—a one day workshop for executive and non-executive directors. Sundridge Park Management Centre.
3. Colin Coulson-Thomas, Competent directors: boardroom myths and realities. *Journal of General Management*, **17** (1), Autumn 1991.
4. Tom Nash, Do these men deliver? *The Director*, October, 1991.
5. J. Beevor, The Role of the Outside Director. A speech to Midland Bank plc, 1979.
6. Greater Authority and Accountability for Non-Executive Directors in Corporate Governance in the 1990s. Merton Associates, performance survey September 1991.
7. Ada Demb and Friedrich Neubauer, *Adding Value with the corporate Board, Perspectives for Managers*. International Institute for Management Development, 1990.
8. *The Arthur Andersen Corporate Register*. Hemmington Scott Publishing Ltd, November 1992.
9. *The Board and the Non-Executive Director: Improving Boardroom Performance*. The PA Consulting Group, 1991.
10. The Working Group on Corporate Governance, A New Compact for Owners and Directors. *Harvard Business Review*, July–August 1991.
11. Allister Wilson, Working for power in the boardroom. *The Times*, 5 March 1992.
12. The Cadbury Committee Report on the Financial Aspects of Corporate Governance. The Stock Exchange, May 1992.
13. Jerry Shively, Confessions of a non-executive. *Financial Times*, 15 July 1991.
14. David Clutterbuck and Susan Kernaghan, *The Phoenix Factor: Lessons for Success from Management Failure*. Weidenfeld & Nicolson, 1990.
15. Sir Peter Walters, Thorn EMI Annual Report for 1991.
16. Helen Kay, Inner City circle holds the key to top boardrooms. *The Sunday Times*, 14 June 1882.
17. Non-Executive Directors: Their Value to Management. A paper prepared for the Law and Parliamentary Committee of The Chartered Institute of Management Accountants (CIMA), August 1992.
18. Remuneration Committees—a survey of current practice. PRO NED in conjunction with The Reward Group, PRO NED 1990.
19. The Annual Report of Grand Metropolitan for 1991.
20. Trade and Industry Committee, Takeovers and Mergers, minutes of evidence, House of Commons, Session 1990–91, London HMSO 226–vii. Wednesday 17 April 1991.

5 What are the legal responsibilities, and what contract should an independent director sign?

THE LEGAL RESPONSIBILITIES

In law, non-executive directors share the same responsibilities and liabilities as any other director. The directors as a body are the 'directing mind' of the company and thus held to be ultimately responsible for everything the company does. In theory, at least (if not, by and large in practice), they can be forbidden to hold directorships if the company behaves illegally, or sued by shareholders if it behaves negligently. As with government, there is an assumption of corporate decision-making unless proven to the contrary. The independent director is, therefore, heavily reliant on the honesty, probity and diligence of an executive team he or she may only meet half a dozen times a year.

So onerous have the legal risks become in the United States, that one prominent commentator suggests that no sane person should consider joining the board of a public company. Writing in the *Harvard Business Review*,[1] William Sahlman maintains that becoming an independent director in the United States exposes a person to potential loss of reputation, financial ruin and endless waste of time in dealing with litigious shareholders. He recommends that executives turn down independent director positions until such time as the law is amended to make litigants fully liable for all the costs of their actions.

The United Kingdom has nowhere near as dangerous an environment as that, but the independent director should be fully aware of his or her responsibilities and should have very good directors' liability cover as part of the contract terms.

The issue was brought dramatically to the fore by a series of letters in *The Times*, the first from Sir Edward Du Cann who wrote:[2]

> Current legislation, however, is a severe discouragement to the acceptance of a non-executive appointment as a director of any company.
>
> The law now makes no distinction between the part-time non-executive director and the full-time executive. Non-executive directors have the responsibility of applying an independent judgement to a company's affairs, but they must rely upon the limited information supplied by management.
>
> If they are now to be held fully accountable at law for a company's trading misfortunes (possibly even for a company's debts), whether responsible for them or not, they are hardly likely to make their experience readily available to industry and par-ticularly to ailing companies, however badly both companies and the national interest, may need it.
>
> The risks involved in accepting a non-executive appointment are now so real, particularly at a time of economic recession when a record number of companies have met difficulties, that they are hardly likely to be acceptable to many of those whose broad experience is so badly needed in the boardroom.

While replying correspondents took issue with Du Cann on whether the risks were indeed putting off good potential independent directors, there was strong agreement on the need for insurance. Wrote Andrew Dykes, managing director of Encon Underwriting Ltd:[3]

> Sir Edward Du Cann is right. The risks of becoming a company director, whether non-executive or not, have increased sub-stantially in recent years and directors need relief from this exposure. One way to achieve this is for the company to purchase insurance against the personal liabilities of its directors.
>
> In 1989 the government recognised this and by section 137 of the Companies Act made clear that companies may purchase such protection on behalf of their boards. Not surprisingly, demand for directors' (and company officers') liability insurance has grown rapidly since then, although the British development of this method of protection is still well behind that in the United States and Canada, where it is estimated that over 90 per cent of all companies purchase it.

The risks are not merely financial, however. The potential for loss of personal reputation—for not recognizing the signs of or preventing the collapse of a public company, for example—is also a matter to consider carefully.

The key areas an independent director should be aware of include:

1 The solvency of the company:
   (a) wrongful trading;
   (b) fraudulent trading.
2 The duties of disclosure imposed on a director under the Companies Act,
3 Conflicts of interest: corporate and personal.
4 Insider dealing and compliance with Stock Exchange rules.
5 Compliance with legal requirements imposed by such statutes as the Environmental Protection Act, the Health and Safety at Work Act, the Data Protection Act.

In practice, the independent director may be less vulnerable in law, simply because he or she lacks knowledge of what is going on and is less involved in operating decisions. The key here is what level of knowledge or involvement could reasonably be expected of an independent director doing his or her job properly.

It is also important to recognize the difference between criminal and civil liability.

Civil liability

The duties of a director are to act honestly and in good faith in the interests of the company, and to use the skill and care reasonably attributable to a person in a like position. They apply as much to an independent director as to an executive director. The former duty (commonly known as the fiduciary duty) which largely imposes negative obligations on the director, i.e. not to act dishonestly, not to exceed the powers conferred upon him or her, not to make secret profits, and will be applied as strictly to the independent director as to the executive. In contrast, the duties of skill and care could be more rigorously applied to the executive director with greater knowledge and experience of the company's affairs than to the independent director.

Criminal liability

This depends on the nature of the offence alleged. Breaches of some statutory requirements, for example under the Companies Act, the Health and Safety at Work Act, constitute criminal offences and attract strict liability. *Proof of any knowledge or complicity is not required.* Other offences in escalating order of seriousness require proof of either some failure to exercise due care (negligence), or recklessness or dishonesty. The liability of an independent director for each of these will depend on the level of his or her involvement and knowledge. Thus an independent director is more likely to be liable where the necessary steps to avoid a breach of the criminal code have not been taken, than to be liable for any fraudulent conduct of company business where actual involvement would need to be established.

If a company is in breach of criminal law, then it is often better for the independent director to be ignorant of what is going on, even though he or she has a legal obligation to know. However, recent changes in the United States may well be reflected in the United Kingdom in due course. The US Sentencing Commission has drawn a clear distinction between reasonable and unreasonable ignorance. In essence, its guidelines reduce the likely penalties where directors have carried out reasonable steps to ensure that illegal behaviour does not occur. These steps include having policies and monitoring performance. Turning a blind eye, or engaging in the business equivalent of Henry II's 'Who will free me of this turbulent priest?', on the other hand, attracts a stronger proportion of the blame—and hence of the penalties.

Few, if any, independent directors have been successfully prosecuted on criminal charges in the United Kingdom. (For example, the only director prosecuted in the Guinness affair was an executive.) However, the dangers from civil liability are potentially much greater. The degree to which the independent directors have exercised their duty of care, is often much less black and white. If the executive directors engage in criminal behaviour, then it may be a reasonable assumption that the independent directors should at least have suspected something was going on; and that, if they did not, they were failing in their duty to ask the right questions and insist on receiving relevant information.

More explanation of the legal requirements and their implications is provided in Appendix 1.

Protecting your back

Some basic ground rules for reducing the potential liabilities, which an independent director can take, include the following:

- Before joining a company, try to assess how well informed the existing directors are about what is going on. What information do they receive and is that adequate to prevent misconduct and/or negligence?
- Ensure that ethical issues are discussed at board level, so that policies are clearly understood.
- Ensure that the board minutes are properly recorded and reflect your actual comments—particularly if these involve requests for information, expressions of concern over specific issues, or disagreement over a particular activity. Where report-backs are required, check back over previous minutes to make sure they are not simply forgotten. Make your own notes of the meeting; compare them to the minutes when they are produced; keep your notes for at least three years.
- Make sure you attend board meetings regularly and are fully briefed. (It is much easier to push a dodgy decision through when independent directors are feeling guilty about not having done their homework.)
- Recognize the difference between business as usual and when the company is engaged in momentous policy issues, such as major acquisitions or takeover battles. At

these times, the independent directors typically become more actively involved and hence more vulnerable legally.

- While it may seem dubious from a moral viewpoint, the courts will normally tend to assess the seriousness of a breach of corporate conduct largely on the amount of money involved or the extent of damage to other parties. The independent director, in his or her role as guardian of corporate morality, should ensure that even minor infractions, involving small amounts of money, are used to discuss policy implications.

- Treasure your independence. The more the independent director is locked into the company structure—for example, through performance-related remuneration or share option schemes—the more he or she will be deemed to be involved, and hence liable.

THE CONTRACT

Given that there is no difference in law between an executive and non-executive director, the latter's contract should be as clear and comprehensive as those of his or her executive colleagues. In practice, because so many independent director positions happen almost by accident, they involve no job specification. So, if they have a contract at all—and many do not—it is brief and of little value in defining each party's expectations. In some cases we have encountered, independent directors did not even receive a formal job offer or letter of appointment. And many of the appointment letters independent directors do receive are simply chatty and vague. (An example of a recommended letter of engagement outlining terms and conditions is included in Appendix 2.)

This haphazard state of affairs is changing as more and more boards recognize the value of a contract:

- To set the ground rules: what the independent director is expected to bring to the board, and the basic terms and conditions.

- To protect the independent director from arbitrary dismissal. If the independent director is to be truly independent, he or she should not have to worry that speaking up might lead to loss of income.
- To focus the independent director's efforts where they will be valued most and set standards of performance required.
- To 'legitimize' the relationship to employees. (A clear description of what the independent director is expected to do helps dispel the perception—common in smaller companies—that the chairman is simply dispensing largesse to cronies and relatives.)

The independent directors in our survey[4] had mixed experience, with just over half of their host companies providing them with a clear contract. Of these, virtually all provided details of salary, but only around 60 per cent spelt out details of length of appointment, roles and responsibilities and period of notice.

In some ways, the contract for an independent director needs even more careful thought and consideration than that for an executive. The executive will normally have a clearly defined job, with readily measurable outputs; the independent director has a much less well-defined role, with relatively few measurable outputs. Creating a model contract is, therefore, difficult, if only because each arrangement is likely to be constructed to fit the particular circumstances, background and personality of the individual involved. None the less, it is possible to outline a number of core elements which ought to appear in a well-prepared contract.

Job description

This can be most easily subdivided into when, what and how.

'When' will normally cover the number of meetings to attend, both board meetings, briefing meetings and other special events, such as the once-a-year weekend-long strategic planning exercises that many boards now engage in. The independent director will also need to spend time preparing for meetings—one estimate, by the Top Pay Research Group,[5] suggests that this will typically require half a day preparing for each day 'on parade' at the company.

The more accurate the estimate of time commitment, the better for both sides. Some companies express a minimum number of days required; others also add a maximum, on the grounds that, beyond a certain point, the independent director becomes too involved to remain independent.

'What' covers the expected contribution of the independent director and should spell out in some detail the key roles he or she will be expected to play and the subcommittees of which he or she will be a member. If, for example, the independent director is to sit on the executive remuneration committee, then the contract will also explain in brief what the duties of that committee are.

This part of the contract may also deal with the responsibilities in specific circumstances, such as succession of the chairman and at the annual general meeting.

'How' will cover the manner, in which performance will be measured. It should also give details of the independent director's rights to information, particularly in the areas of finance, corporate governance, pension fund administration and so on.

Fees

The fees of independent directors are normally set by the chairman, in consultation with executive directors and external advisers, although in a small proportion of cases (about 10 per cent according to the Top Pay Research Group) the independent directors consider their own fees.

The contract should specify what the basic fee rate is, and how it is set. It should also explain what other moneys the independent director is entitled to claim—for example, travel and accommodation expenses. It might also establish a basis for additional payments if the independent director puts in considerable excess hours on behalf of the company. Some independent directors have arrangements that allow them to charge a daily fee (say £1500) for time over and above the basic allocation. One of the benefits of such arrangements is that they may feel less constrained about giving extra time at crisis periods, when it is needed.

In practice, independent directors do not normally receive very large basic fees. The Top Pay Research Group found that the profile of basic fees paid by companies of different sizes was remarkably flat, as Table 5.1 indicates.

Table 5.1   *Basic fees for independent directors, 1990*

Company turnover (£000,000)	Lower quartile (£'000s)	Median quartile (£'000s)	Upper quartile (£'000s)
20–150	5	5–10	10–15
150–300	5–10	10–15	10–15
300–500	5–10	10–15	10–15
500–1000	5–10	10–15	15–20
1000 +	5–10	10–15	15–20

Source: Top Pay Research Group.

Within the figures in Table 5.1 lie numerous variations of time and commitment. An independent chairman spending six days a month in the company would typically receive rather more, for example. Subcommittee chairmen also typically receive a modest extra level of fees to cover the greater responsibility.

The tenor of many reports on independent director compensation is that fee levels are too low. For example, the 1991 study by Merton Associates states:[6] 'Fees shall be increased to adequately reflect the importance of the function—at present they do not.' However, there is a counter argument that it is better to pay a relatively modest fee than to undermine the independent director's independence by making the position overly important in terms of the individual's income. While the fee should be adequate to attract the right calibre of person, it should not be so generous as to buy the independent director's freedom of thought and expression.

One line of argument suggests that any potential independent director, who insists upon a fee basis beyond the norm, is unlikely to be sufficiently committed to the organization. People with a string of independent directorships may be the most likely to make such demands, because of the opportunity cost of sitting on one board as compared to another. The perceptive chairman will consider carefully just how much value for money he is likely to receive in such circumstances.

We expect the pressure for higher fees for independent directors to increase in the rest of this decade. On the one hand, a variety of interested bodies is pushing the notion that independent directors are underpaid, albeit with little evidence to support their assertions. On the other, one of the influences of the Cadbury Report,[7] which promotes a more professional approach to choosing and using independent directors, will be increasing disfavour towards multiple independent directorships. Just because people are discouraged from holding more than one independent directorship, it does not necessarily follow that they should expect to be paid more for that position, to compensate for their loss. If they are paid more, it should be on the basis of a significantly increased contribution.

It is also worth noting here that in many cases independent directors do not personally receive their fees, which are paid instead to their primary employer, as a partial reimbursement of time and costs. Independent directors from professional practices will most commonly operate in this manner.

In our survey,[4] we also asked about perks as part of the remuneration package. Only four companies provided independent directors with cars. Slightly less than half provided directors' liability insurance—but, significantly, most of those independent directors had liability insurance for each of the boards on which they served. The implication here is that, if the individual independent director requires it, companies will agree. Those independent directors, who do not receive director's liability insurance are exposed to a much higher risk, which is unlikely to be compensated for in other parts of the remuneration package.

Very few independent directors had share options as part of their package, while membership of the company private healthcare scheme was even less common (probably at least partially because they would have been members of their own company's scheme).

The issue of share options is closely allied to that of performance bonuses. In theory, if the independent directors share the responsibilities for directing the company, they should also share in the rewards for success. If executive directors can achieve share options and bonuses, why should independent directors not receive the same?

In practice, however, the compensation packages offered to executive and independent directors are and have to be fundamentally different, because the psychology and motivational drive of their jobs is different. Executive incentives are designed to make things happen—they are a reward as much for implementation as for effective planning. Non-executives have little input to this process—their contribution comes from questioning, stimulating and monitoring.

To attempt to incentivize both executives and independent directors with the same reward schemes is a symptom of the muddled thinking that afflicts so much of the discussion about non-executive roles. That is not to say that independent directors cannot be incentivized, but the incentives must be directly related to the specific expectations the company has of them in their specific role.

A further important issue in the area of compensation is severance pay or golden handshakes. If the appointment does not work out, then arguably the company is as much to blame as the independent director. Terms of separation need to be clearly spelt out and should be sufficiently generous not to penalize the independent director unduly for speaking his or her mind.

Severance pay also comes to the fore in the case of a takeover attempt. If it is successful, the independent directors are at least as likely as the executives to lose their jobs. While the loss to the executives is clearly greater, some compensation should be built in. If the board wishes to make the scale of compensation penal against would-be predators, then so-called 'golden parachutes' for the independent directors could also be included.

Administrative support

If the independent director has a specific role, such as chairman of the remuneration subcommittee, he or she will need administrative back up. This may take the form of office space, secretarial help, expert external advice or even, in extreme cases, a small staff. (In the latter case, the distinction between executive and non-executive would become very blurred.) The non-executive chairman of a large public limited company may require a chauffeured car. Even the independent director without portfolio will have some need of support services. The contract should specify how these are to be paid for and provided.

In many cases, the independent director absorbs these administrative expenses within his or her normal job, only claiming for personal out-of-pocket expenses, such as travel. In other cases, the company must decide whether it wants to provide administrative support directly, or to fund the independent director to acquire it from outside. The latter alternative frequently works out much cheaper and has the additional benefit that the independent director has control of his own administrative processes.

Contract period

Companies change. People change. Competencies and networks become obsolete. For all these reasons and many more, no appointment of an independent director should be without a clearly defined contract period. Sir Adrian Cadbury expresses the point this way: 'I'm convinced that, after a time, almost imperceptibly, an outsider becomes an insider and that edge of independence that is so important is slightly blunted—so I think you need to have a process of renewal. The fixed term [contract] gives you a way to do that.'

There is, of course, a fundamental paradox here. On the one hand, it is clearly wrong to have an open-ended contract, where people continue to serve until they drop and half the board makes only 5 per cent of the contribution. Yet a fixed term itself restricts the independent director's independence, because it is all too easy to fall into the trap of not making waves at the moment because the time for contract renewal is coming up again.

Nevertheless, the most sensible answer seems to be to have renewable contracts, regularly reviewed. Naturally, however, opinions vary about the period for which contracts should run. For example, Michael Jackaman, the chairman of Allied Lyons, favours a three-year appointment of non-executive directors, with an option of renewing the term for another three years. Our research suggests, however, that an annually renewable contract has much to recommend it.

It also makes sense to apply a retirement age to independent directors, suggests Sir Colin Southgate, chairman of Thorn EMI. Quite what that limit should be, and what exceptions should be allowed, will depend on each company's circumstances, but most managers will already have begun to retire mentally by 65 and their networks will have become largely obsolete within two years after that. (On the other hand, there are many very effective independent directors well into their seventies. William Shaw, former finance director of BAA declares at 64 that he has not found his first real challenge yet!)

Performance assessment

If independent directors are to be effective, they need to know how they are doing. Business consultant John Cheele puts the point that the chairman : 'should carry out an annual review for his non-executives, just as he would do a staff appraisal for other employees of the company'.

The contract should state clearly when the review will take place, who will be involved and what measurements of performance will be examined. It should also state whether and how this will be linked to remuneration.

Conflict of interest

Any areas of potential or actual conflict of interest should have been identified long before the contract is drawn up.

However, it is important for the contract to record these and how they are to be handled if they arise.

Conflict of opinion

The contract should be explicit on the independent director's rights and responsibilities in these circumstances. The Institute of Director's Code of Practice[8] provides a useful and apposite form of words for this purpose, which companies may wish to adopt verbatim:

> The non-executive's primary intention is clearly to make an objective and constructive contribution towards the effective direction of the company's affairs. Such intention implies working within the framework of the board to resolve conflicts of opinion, personality or policy.
>
> It is, however, understood that the non-executive director may take such individual action, including resignation, as he or she considers the company's interest demands if:
> a)   the board persists in a course of action which is believed to be contrary to the interests of the company
> b)   the board will not take steps to correct what are believed to be unacceptable irregularities within the company.
>
> In both instances, the points at issue will have been previously raised and discussed during one or more scheduled meetings of the board at which the non-executive has attended and made his or her opinions known.

Arbitration

A basic arbitration clause is a practical precaution in any contract. While it would be wrong to go into a relationship expecting problems (rather like sorting out the divorce arrangements at the wedding registry office), having a clear process to resolve disputes saves a great deal of rancour and executive time. The clause should specify under what circumstances arbitration will be used, how the arbitrator will be chosen (or who the arbitrator will be) and the steps that must be gone through before arbitration is invoked.

Miscellaneous items

There will often be a number of minor items relating to the specific circumstances of the company or the top team. Increasingly common, for example, is a requirement for all directors to purchase a minimum number or value of shares, as a sign of commitment to the organization.

Opinions are strongly divided on the advisability of independent directors having shares. While participation in ownership may increase commitment, it also reduces independence. Comments Kep Simpson:

> Unfortunately, most independent directors are not altruistic when it comes to the crunch. That's one of the reasons why I have reservations about independent directors holding shares. There is perhaps a case for a company that takes its independent directors seriously to set up a trust fund, out of which they are paid and to buffer them from any decisions they might make.

With all these elements included, the contract can amount to a relatively lengthy document. For neither party should the aim be to tie the other down to a tight deal, however. The detail is necessary to make sure that each understands the nature of the obligations to the other. For that reason, while the document should be vetted by a lawyer, we strongly recommend that it be written in simple, readily understandable English, rather than legalese.

It also helps to encapsulate some of the more day-to-day, practical aspects of the role in an accompanying letter. This can go into detail on issues such as the following:

- Induction requirements: what kind of induction he or she should take part in and when.
- Introducing the independent director to his or her new colleagues (perhaps through an enclosed set of CVs).
- Dates of all planned meetings he or she will be expected to attend over the following six months.
- Minor perks, such as employee discount schemes, to which the independent director is entitled.

The letter should also draw the independent director's attention to key elements of the contract and specify a date, by which it should be returned signed. It should also offer an opportunity for the independent director to talk the details through with the chairman or chief executive.

While the contract must of necessity be a formal, relatively cold document, the accompanying letter should be warm, welcoming and relatively informal, even though legally it is all part of the job offer.

If all this sounds a little bureaucratic, that is not unusual when previously haphazard processes are brought under control. The urgent need over the coming decade is to professionalize the role of independent director. A well-managed approach to contract generation is at least a start.

SUMMARY

Although many independent directors are appointed without a contract, legal liability alone suggests that it makes sense on both sides to be very clear about the nature of the appointment and the terms of the agreement. After all, if the appointment really is important to the strategy of the company, then it should be made in as professional a manner as possible.

REFERENCES

1. William Sahlman, Why sane people shouldn't serve on public boards. *Harvard Business Review*, May–June 1990.
2. Sir Edward Du Cann, writing in a letter to *The Times*, 9 October 1991.
3. Andrew Dykes, also in a letter to *The Times*, writing in reply to Edward Du Cann's letter, 14 October 1991.
4. Making the most of Non-Executive Directors—a survey by Hanson Green and The ITEM Group plc, 1992.
5. Remuneration Committees: An Update of Current Practice. A survey carried out by Top Pay Research Group. The Foundation for Business Responsibilities, 1991.
6. Greater Authority and Accountability for Non-Executive Directors in Corporate Governance in the 1990s. Merton Associates, performance survey September 1991.
7. The Cadbury Committee Report on the Financial Aspects of Corporate Governance. The Stock Exchange, May 1992.
8. Code of Practice for the Non-Executive Director. The Institute of Directors (undated) and *Guidelines for Directors*, 5th edn. Institute of Directors, September 1991.

6 Choosing and using independent directors

In this chapter, which is aimed primarily at chief executives and controlling shareholders, you will encounter a number of messages which, assuming you have read the previous chapters, you will already have encountered. The reason, quite simply, is that here we bring them together in a step-by-step approach towards gaining a cadre of effective, motivated and valued independent directors.

We have advanced a variety of reasons why independent directors so often fail to add value, but ultimately these all owe their origins to lack of clarity on the part of both executive management and the independent directors as to precisely what is expected of the role. The PA study[1] found that 60 per cent of companies appoint non-executive directors without defining what they should do. If independent directors are to prevent themselves from being marginalized or otherwise rendered ineffective, they need to obtain a clear definition of what they are expected to do.

In many cases, the lack of clarity or purpose is a symptom of a deeper malaise—a fundamental inadequacy of vision of the board itself. Too many boards have little real sense of what they are there to do, or why; what the proper direction of their energies should be; what the outcome of their deliberations should be; what are proper and improper topics for them to discuss; what obligations they owe to the various stakeholders. In such an environment, the only real benefits likely to flow from an independent director is that he or she may have the perspicacity to cut through the obfuscation and insist on bringing some order and vision to the gathering.

At the other extreme, we encounter companies where the

executives perceive the appointment of an independent director as a panacea for the multiple ills of the organization. This is equally untenable. The nature of major change demands that an insider drives it; an independent director can only do so by abandoning his or her independent status.

We have also seen banks and investment institutions appoint seasoned, heavyweight executives as independent directors to unruly and undisciplined boards of entrepreneurial companies—to sort them out. Leaving aside the question of capability of some of these appointments, such an approach often runs into trouble because it is the equivalent of using an axe where a rapier would be far more effective. Similarly, building societies that have amassed large teams of independent directors (much on the lines of the governing council of a professional body) are confusing quantity with quality.

There is, of course, no such thing as an ideal board, because every company's requirements and circumstances will differ. However, as a very general statement of good practice, we suggest that a board should achieve a balance between compactness, for rapid, consensus-led decision-making, and having enough people to present a variety of alternative views on important issues. For a small company, the ideal size is probably about six, with at least two being independent directors; for a large company, no more than a dozen, of whom four would be independent directors. (More than a dozen and it becomes extremely difficult to mould together a team. Rugby clubs only manage to create teams of 15 players by spending a great deal of time together, practising—a luxury most boards do not have.)

On balance, our ideal board would have a non-executive chairman and a strong chief executive able to run the company on a day-to-day basis without having to report back constantly. The various board members, both executive and independent, would range in age from early forties to late sixties and be drawn from different backgrounds and disciplines. Without falling prey to tokenism, the board would also include women and ethnic minorities and at least one independent director from another European country.

The independent directors would be in the majority on the

executive compensation committee. One or more would also take the role of company representative on the pension fund; one would act as ombudsman, receiving and investigating complaints of malpractice and raising ethical issues. All would sit on the audit committee.

Although such an ideal board is likely to be a rare bird, the closer a company can come to the ideal, the clearer directors—both executive and independent—are likely to be about their roles and the more likely they are to deliver real value.

The three key stages in acquiring effective independent directors are as follows:

- *Defining the role*: what precisely do you want the independent director to do?
- *Searching for and selecting the right candidate.*
- *Induction.*

DEFINING THE ROLE: WHAT PRECISELY DO YOU WANT THE INDEPENDENT DIRECTOR TO DO?

The simple answer to the question—we hope—is that you want the independent director to add value. The critical issue is 'how?'

In Chapter 2, we explored a range of ways in which independent directors can add value. Some of these will be relevant to your organization and its current needs; some may not. By defining at the start precisely the inputs and outputs you require, you both make the search easier and increase the chances of a successful appointment.

Do not just rely on your own perceptions about the nature of the job. Involve other executives and, if possible, some of the managers in the layer below. Also seek advice from other informed observers, such as management consultants, who have worked closely with the company, key customers and your auditors or solicitors. Make a point also of talking to other chief executives or chairmen about how they select candidates, and to independent directors of other companies. Putting together their various perceptions will enable you to develop a picture with much greater depth.

Says one observer: 'The process for selecting independent directors must include a Board-level discussion of the qualities that are required. Often it will be to fill gaps in the knowledge and experience of the board. Once the requirements have been defined, it's best to hand the search process over to an executive search company.'

Key questions might include:

- What kinds of challenges/insights are we looking for?
- How much time are we expecting this person to devote to the job?
- Are we looking for support in any of the functional areas, or simply a broad input of wisdom?
- Will the person have special responsibilities towards any particular group of stakeholders (e.g. banks, institutional investors)?
- Is this individual to be a potential future independent chairperson?
- Which subcommittees of the board will the person be a member of?

Having assessed the role, you can now start to define the characteristics of the ideal candidate. Again, you should enlist the thoughts of a wide circle of interested observers. Key questions to consider include:

- What experience are we looking for?
- What personality traits?
- Which personal strengths are critical, which are important and which are of minor or no importance?
- Does he or she need any special functional competencies (e.g. legal or financial knowledge)?
- How should this person affect the balance and 'fit' of the team? (Should he or she change it or reinforce it and why?)

Inevitably, as soon as you begin to ask people such questions, they will start to put together a mental picture of their own preferred candidate and probably offer a few names from their own network of contacts. It is important to resist the temptation to pursue these leads until you have a very clear picture and a degree of consensus on the nature of the job and the ideal person to fill it.

Two notes of caution here, however. One is to be very careful not to become so prescriptive in identifying your ideal candidate that you exclude non-standard candidates who might actually provide greater value. The other is to temper your criteria with one final consideration: 'How am I going to get on with this person?' A clash of personality between the chief executive and independent directors is one of the most destructive things that can happen to a board.

The experience of the chief executive of a consultancy company, set up by a business school, found himself saddled with a team of independent directors with whom he had little in common. He declares: 'I often find myself wondering why they are there, except to interfere. We grew the company 70 per cent last year, against a recession, but it was largely in spite of the non-executives.' Not surprisingly, relationships became increasingly strained, leading him to re-examine his career direction.

In thinking through what you want independent directors for, you must be as honest as possible with yourself and try to involve other people in the process. One of the main reasons for poor appointments is that arrogant and dominant chairmen or chief executives control the whole process of appointing independent directors. Sometimes their appointments are to repay a favour to a powerful colleague (you scratch my back and I'll scratch yours); sometimes they simply want to pack the board with cronies they can rely on to support the chairman's line.

Another unpromising reason for appointing independent directors is to respond to pressure from institutional shareholders, concerned about the chairman/CEO's dictatorial style or about the organization's public image. If the chairman/CEO makes the appointments himself or herself, the likelihood is that these independent directors will be anything but critical of policy. If the independent directors are selected by the institutions, there is likely to be rapid and growing friction within the board, adding further to the company's troubles. In such cases, the investors must be prepared to use the independent directors to assess the extent of the problems caused by the chairman/CEO and, if these are sufficiently severe, remove him or her from office. Track record suggests that institutions are more likely to allow the situation to drift indefinitely, although the recession of the early 1990s has seen a general toughening up in this respect.

RESEARCHING AND SELECTING CANDIDATES

Writing down the descriptions of the job and likely suitable candidates provides a useful checklist for reviewing your conclusions with other people (this *is* the time to ask them who they know, who might fit the profile). It also gives candidates a very clear yardstick, against which to measure themselves. Moreover, if you decide to use a headhunter or specialist independent director search consultancy, you can avoid a great deal of initial discussion of your objectives and requirements.

In practice, many companies still do not apply any rigorous procedures to selection. A survey by the Stock Exchange and PRO NED in mid–1992[2] revealed that about half of independent directors had simply been appointed on the nomination of the company chairman and fewer than a quarter of companies had prepared a job profile in advance.

There are a number of obvious routes to identify suitable candidates. For example, there are the formal lists maintained by PRO NED, the Institute of Directors, 3i and some other investment institutions, and a handful of specialist headhunters. The problem with such formal lists is that they tend to reflect the *status quo*. Many excellent candidates simply will not be on them.

Identifying such people requires extensive and time-consuming networking. (We haven't yet encountered a company that advertises vacancies for independent directors, but no doubt that will come.) Some of the women's networks, such as Women in Management, will have within them people who know everyone, and who will be more than willing to make introductions. Independent management consultants, business journalists, public relations specialists

and similar observers are often likely to provide some unexpected but valuable suggestions and introductions. Banks
and accountants, often the first port of call for CEOs hunting
independent directors, have a poor overall record, in our
experience, in making such recommendations (let alone
making independent director appointments to companies in
their own care). So, too, do venture capitalists, whose often
uninspired and uninspiring appointees can all too easily stifle
the entrepreneurial spirit of companies being nurtured by
staying too long.

Other useful networks to tap into include industry federations, charities, theatre trusts, NHS Trusts, Training and
Enterprise Councils and so on, where business people mix
with people from other backgrounds. While most appointments to these bodies may still be from the Great and the
Good, there will be a spread of interesting people with both
something to offer and practical experience in an equivalent
role to independent director. An NHS Trust, for example,
may employee several thousand people and have a budget
the size of a medium-sized company.

The better the idea you have of the qualities you are
looking for, the more easily you will be able to clear a path
through the smog of conflicting recommendations.

Once the search process has been underway for a week or
two, you should review the early results with two key
questions:

- Is the overall calibre of the people we are encountering at
  about the right level?
- Are we obtaining a sufficiently wide spread of backgrounds and experience?

The latter point is critical if we are to develop a national pool
of experienced and effective independent directors—to open
a new deck rather than simply shuffle the existing one. (After
all, the easiest route of all to find an independent director is to
approach someone who already serves in the same capacity
on another board.) Comments headhunter Douglas Kinnaird
in the magazine *Scottish Business Insider*:

Invariably these days, clients who are on the non-executive director recruitment trail are insisting that they don't want someone
from the 'circuit'. But there's a conundrum here: they may have
no desire to take on those who have 10, 20 or even more directorship scalps on their belts—but they do want some reassurance
about the track record. 'If nobody else wants them', they'll moan,
'I'm not sure if I do' ... The real dream is to find an executive
achiever who is doing extremely well, who has been with the
organization for 5–7 years, who is on top of his job, who is
well-rewarded—and who is bored. Such people need excitement;
they need stimulation; they need variety. Frequently that means
they need change. If their existing function cannot provide it,
well—when the call comes from us, they move. I suggest—that a
company often stands a better chance of hanging on to prized
performers like this by encouraging them to undertake new
external challenges of the sort implied by non-executive directorships.

Important sources for non-standard independent directors

Women

A study carried out several years ago by one of the authors[3]
compared the careers of women who had reached senior
positions within large companies and women who had succeeded as entrepreneurs. It found a strong correlation
between whether women found a senior management
mentor and whether they quit to set up on their own, frustrated at lack of opportunity to prove themselves. Women
entrepreneurs have often learnt harder and more significant
lessons than their male equivalents and can often, therefore,
bring more to the board discussions.

The toughest and most effective entrepreneurs can be invaluable in questioning received wisdom on a wide variety of
issues, from employment policy to environmental protection
and company image—often with a directness many male
colleagues would hesitate to use. Such managers should be
considered in their own right as shortlist candidates; never
added as token gestures. Where possible, they should not be
placed in the uncomfortable position of being the only

woman on the board, because that may inhibit the very expression of originality and perceptiveness that you wish to encourage.

Those women who do become independent directors often find that they have to keep a very disciplined diary, planning weeks and months ahead, to fulfil their independent director responsibilities. Having made the commitment, however, they are frequently much more diligent about keeping it than many of their male colleagues.

Investment fund managers

Considering how much time these people spend talking to chairmen, it is amazing how few of them find their way on to boards. Yet if part of the role of the board is to maintain and/or increase share price, it surely makes sense to have that expertise within the board team.

European managers

When seeking an input of Euro-knowledge on to the board, many companies opt for a British manager who has extensive expatriate experience. There is no shortage of businesspeople who have worked in a particular country or can claim instant knowledge of an important emerging foreign economy. While this can be useful, it is in reality a feeble half-measure, and no substitute for the real thing. No British businessman or woman will understand the foreign culture so well, or speak the language so intuitively as to be able to get under the skin of the other country. (Look at the number of European and US managers who lived and worked in Japan yet failed to understand the competitive strategy of Japanese companies.) Perhaps the best possible combination is to have both a British non-executive director with knowledge of the area, supported by a local businessman or woman from the country concerned.

Diplomats

Preferably before they gain their knighthoods and become functionally obsolete. The company that negotiates frequently with overseas governments can find insights at this level very useful. On the other hand, it may not be a good idea to appoint a diplomat for his or her contacts, except in the short term, because they can rapidly become outdated. Another cautionary factor is that most diplomats, who enter the commercial world, do so fairly late in life—they are unlikely to be at their prime.

The military

This category can be more attractive, being generally somewhat younger at retirement. They are used to running a big defence business, know how Whitehall works, and have strong organizational, logistics and presentation skills. However, there may be big gaps in their business knowledge.

Lawyers

Lawyers are a much underutilized source. The top professionals can master a brief, ask intelligent, penetrating questions and are increasingly used to running relatively large businesses, now that so many legal practices have merged into substantial operations with several hundred employees or partners. Their network of contacts is also valuable.

One of the principal benefits from having a lawyer on board is to help ensure that the executives stay within the law and to take an independent, broader look at the company than an in-house legal department would typically be able to do. Another is to deflate some of the arrogance, with which some professional advisers treat their clients, by asking the questions that reveal the thin patches in a presentation. It is much harder to pull the wool over the eyes of another professional.

Design company top management

They may also have a useful perspective to offer in manufacturing companies. Would the UK motorcycle industry have collapsed as rapidly as it did, for example, if there had been someone at the top of companies asking the pertinent questions about design issues?

Merchant bankers

Through their knowledge of international finance, they can bring a valuable extra dimension to board deliberations. They can also act as a bridge between the company and the City. Such an appointment can be particularly effective for a company, unused to the nuances of high finance, which recognizes the shortcoming in its board's composition.

Alternatively, it may be seen as a way to forge closer links inside the Square Mile. For example, *The Financial Times* viewed Allied Lyons' recent appointment of Miles Rivett-Carnac—deputy chairman of Barings—as a non-executive director as 'continuing to mend its fences with the City'.

There is potential for conflict of interest in the appointment of merchant bankers as independent directors. In the case of Rivett-Carnac, however, Allied Lyons' chairman, Michael Jackaman, stresses that Barings is not retained as his company's permanent financial adviser. Given that Rivett-Carnac is close to retirement, Jackaman thinks there is no conflict of interest in having the chairman of one of the City's bigger fund managers on his board.

Public relations

As an industry, PR also contains a number of highly perceptive minds, used to identifying critical issues and analysing the impact of public perceptions. Advice at board level can assist in getting best value out of PR suppliers.

Business academics

They also have a very different perspective. Part of their value is keeping the board up-to-date with latest thinking on strategic planning and management. Unlike management consultants, they do not necessarily have the conflict of interest of wanting to sell you the services of their organization. Again, they will have knowledge of best practice in a wide spread of organizations and the analytical ability to look at business problems in new ways.

One of the authors, for instance, appointed Professor Keith Macmillan, deputy principal of Henley Management College, as an independent director for Canon UK. He was appropriate as a confidant to the Japanese chairman, who, despite having been in the United Kingdom for a number of years, welcomed a relationship with a professor from a first class business school, responsible for the MBA programme, with some experience of running his own firm and used to running brainstorming sessions for companies.

Another recent appointment by the same source was also more hybrid than it appeared. When Sir John Banham, then about to retire as CBI director general at the tender age of 50, was appointed independent chairman of the venture capital firm, Equity Capital for Industry (ECI) a number of factors were taken into account by all concerned.

The timing of the appointment was important. With the somewhat tentative prospect of an economic upturn, the ECI platform was attractive. It was also different from the other post-CBI appointments which he had already accepted, including the public appointment (to review the reorganization of local government) and the non-executive directorships of major public limited companies. Together, these factors made him an ideal candidate and an ideal match. And that was without allowing for his first class network.

However, not every independent director is in favour of enlarging the pool of candidates to include non-business persons. Says one observer: 'I find it difficult to see how experience in the voluntary sector or diplomatic service is relevant. Experience of government is of course relevant to certain companies. In brief it is more important to widen the circle of quality independent business related directors than it is to bring in people from a non-business background.'

A constrasting view is taken by Sir Nigel Mobbs, chairman of Slough Estates and independent director of Barclays Bank, Kingfisher and Cookson Holdings: 'We have had great success in appointing non-executive directors from a non-business background, particularly those who have government experience. Again it is important to select the candidate carefully, based upon his previous experience and his personality to ensure that he fits into the board culture.'

Other sources

On the other side of the coin are those groups, whom it is best to discount, or at least treat with extreme caution as potential independent directors.

Politicians

Politicians rarely have much practical business experience, no matter what they claim. What experience they do have is usually limited to a superficial knowledge of companies in their constituencies or as a result of their ministerial portfolio. Even those with a genuine business background are unlikely to have kept their commercial edge after a decade in the House of Commons. The most common reason for appointing MPs as independent directors seems to be to make use of their influence in the House and in Whitehall.

The aristocracy

They can still be seen on the boards of companies, but increasingly less so. Relatively few bring any useful management expertise, and those that do tend to have had some exposure to financial disciplines. Those appointed from some misguided sense of status (nobody now believes that having a peer or two on the board confers any sense of increased financial probity and soundness) often struggle to keep up with the demands of the job in the late twentieth century.

Management consultants

They do not usually make good independent directors. Not only do they find it difficult to separate the selling role from the directorial role, but the two roles are different both legally and psychologically. Part of the role of a consultant is not to become involved to the extent of taking responsibility for decisions, only for the quality of advice offered; yet an independent director has no choice but to take responsibility.

Kep Simpson highlights the distinction between consultancy and independent directorship: 'In practice, being a Board colleague does make a difference from being a consultant. As a consultant, you are always treated as an outsider. The independent director is like the member of a club, although it is expected your viewpoint will be different.'

Management consultants can often be highly effective when they are no longer practising; and on the boards of other forms of consulting organizations.

If you do hire a consultant and wish him or her to have access to board deliberations, then permit him or her to attend as an observer. This can be particularly useful if you wish to gain an external view on how to improve the effectiveness of board meetings. Alternatively, if you really want to include a consultant on the board, make it part of the terms and conditions that your company cannot maintain a trading relationship with the consultancy at any other level. The uncommitted individual is likely to fade away rapidly at that point!

Customers and suppliers

Because they have a trading relationship with your company, they can never be fully independent.

Local dignitaries

They may occasionally be able to help with planning permissions, but it is often difficult to see what other value they can bring to the board by virtue of their local government experience. However, the chief executive of a large local council certainly has responsibility for running a large and complex business, and in theory his supervisory board consists of the councillors.

Many local dignitaries, who become independent directors, come to rely on the salary, making them even less likely to put forward alternative views at board meetings.

Bank managers

Bank managers, even at very senior levels in City or regional headquarters, tend to fall into the customer/supplier category. They also have the curious handicap that their own boards are often too large, include former executives as independent directors, and generally have an amateurish, illogical air about their composition. The average age is also higher than it should be. Yet they tend to demand a high calibre of independent director on client company boards where they have a strong influence and, given their highly regulated environment, should have a relatively good understanding of the issues.

Directors of recently privatized companies

They may have been appointed from within and may not have shed the attitudes ingrained by years of working in a monopolistic, bureaucratic organization. The selection of independent directors for some of these companies (particularly the utilities) at the time of privatization also left a great deal to be desired.

Our survey indicates that selection of independent directors is still a relatively undisciplined process. For example, one-third said that the role they were expected to play was not clearly defined by either the company or themselves.

Another generally poor source of independent directors is people who have recently retired from the company, or are about to do so—as a sort of retirement present.

Says former Legal & General chief executive Joe Palmer: 'Legal & General has a policy of the "clean break" for executives. I supported that policy as an executive. Anecdotal evidence from companies which do retain retired executives on boards strongly confirms that the disadvantages powerfully outweigh any advantages.'

Adds MEPC's Jim Beveridge: 'I believe it is wrong to make former executive directors of the company non-executive directors following their retirement. Non-executive directors should bring independent fresh ideas into the company.'

However, there are exceptions to the rule. David O'Shaugnessy, an executive director of Metal Box before its merger with the French company Carnaud, stayed on with the new company and eventually became an independent director on the French supervisory board in October 1992. Part of the logic behind retaining him in the company was to strengthen the packaging industry knowledge at supervisory board level. He explains: 'The supervisory tier currently has two accountants, one strategy development director, a chairman and chief executive of another company with a packaging subsidiary, and an ex-CMB main board director. My addition will strengthen the knowledge of the industry and the company on the supervisory Board.'

In this particular case, the supervisory board is made up entirely of independent directors, so some knowledge of the company and the markets is essential to structure board discussions. The directoire, which reports to the supervisory board, is made up entirely of executives.

The unusual nature of the case does not mean that the potential problems of conflict of role can be ignored, however. O'Shaugnessy bluntly admits: 'I think the toughest part of my new role as an independent director will probably be to keep my hands off the executive tiller.'

Equally, an independent directorship should not be a reward for faithful service or a means of locking in key people.

MAKING THE APPROACH

The initial approach to a potential independent director should always be informal. Some CEOs prefer to adopt the classic headhunters' approach of contacting the executive first to enquire if he or she could recommend anyone for the post. This has the advantage that both parties can discuss the issue at arm's length, and are able to withdraw without embarrassment. In many ways it is like being a prospective parliamentary candidate—an official declaration of intent needs to be suspended until the picture becomes clearer.

The potential independent director will need a copy of the outline description of the job and of the ideal candidate. In discussing round these descriptions, you can rapidly gain an insight into the individual's background, experience, personality and likely degree of fit within the existing team.

Before taking the discussions any further, you need to generate a formal shortlist, comparing the most suitable candidates against the requirements. Simply ticking off each attribute on a checklist will not provide an accurate picture, because some attributes are more important than others. A more practical method is to weight each characteristic according to importance.

The final scores you assign to each candidate will inevitably contain a degree of guesswork, so you should not simply take the top candidate as the obvious winner, unless there is a clear gap of at least 15–20 per cent. Normally you will have a small cluster of front runners, whom you need to investigate more thoroughly. Before doing so, however, you should look at the profile of these people. Are they *too* similar in background or personality type? If they are, could that be because the selection criteria are too rigid or wrongly weighted? Or does it accurately reflect the availability of suitable candidates?

Now you need to get down to brass tacks with the people on the shortlist. You may already have had an informal meeting with them, probably over lunch away from their office and yours. Some chairmen use this next meeting as an opportunity to meet the individual on his or her own ground, taking the view that you can pick up a lot of clues about someone's standing and experience from their own working environment. Others prefer to invite the person to lunch at the host company's offices, where there is an opportunity for several executives to meet him or her and develop an opinion. The critical requirement is to hold the meeting in an environment that encourages frank and forthright discussion on both sides.

With very few exceptions, executives are not trained as professional job interviewers. So it makes sense to involve other directors and advisers in the interview. Not only may they have a different perspective from your own, but they give you someone to discuss your thoughts with subsequently. However, the special nature of the independent director relationship and the status attached to it, mean that many candidates would take unkindly to an obvious interview panel. The overtone of the meeting needs to be much more a relaxed exchange of opinions and general getting to know each other than a barrage of questions; the undertone is a mutually understood agenda of information exchange about the candidate and the company.

You should, however, expect the candidate to have thought through how he or she will be able to bring added value to the board, and to explain this articulately. If you have not already provided them, he or she should at the very least have asked for or otherwise acquired some background on the company—for example, the annual report and any recent reviews by brokers' analysts.

Some people will rule themselves out at this stage, through unexpected conflicts of interest, unacceptable personality traits, or a feeling on your part that they are already over the hill. (For the latter, simply listen to the language people use: is it dynamic and forward-looking, or passive and nostalgic?) Others will simply decide that they are not interested. For those who remain, you will probably require at least a couple of further meetings, probably with different people from the board. These meetings serve a dual function. Not only do they increase the body of people who can take a view on the candidate, but they help him or her acquire a broader knowledge of the organization.

The final selection is rarely easy. In spite of all the consensus-gathering we have urged, the chairman/CEO must ultimately make the appointment and there will be times when he or she correctly overrides the doubts of individual executive colleagues. That said, the greater the degree of agreement around the table that a candidate is 'right' for the post, the more likely the candidate is to fit in.

It may also become clear, at the end of the day, that none of the candidates is really right. The temptation is to appoint the best of the bunch. If you do so, you are effectively saying that the independent director position is relatively unimportant, that it does not matter if it is occupied by someone not quite up to the job. While the individual concerned may well grow into the job, the stigma has already been planted and will be very difficult to expunge.

Equally, you may find that you have two (or more) superb candidates, from whom you must more or less arbitrarily select one. If the other candidates are that good, however, can you afford not to invite them on to your board? If they, too, can bring great added value, surely it is a waste not to take advantage of their talent? After all, by now they should already have accumulated a useful knowledge of the company. While the chairman will not wish to overburden the board with independent directors, he or she should at least consider whether the benefits of another, unplanned appointment will outweigh the disadvantages.

WHO SHOULD CHOOSE THE NEW INDEPENDENT DIRECTOR?

Both our researches and years of experience of non-executive appointments (one of the authors works full-time in the field of non-executive recruitment) reveal a wide disparity of views on this topic, with some people arguing strongly for the executives, others for the independent directors to make the selection. One area of relative agreement is that the chairman (whether executive or non-executive) should not make the appointment on his own.

Gordon Owen maintains: 'There should be something in the code of best corporate governance which prevents the chairman appointing his own non-executive directors without prior consultation with the whole Board. Surprisingly in practice this rarely happened.'

Says Sir Alick Rankin, chairman of Scottish & Newcastle plc:

> Today, no chairman can afford to place himself in a position where the independence of his relationship with his non-executive directors could be questioned.
>
> If any shareholder were to ask the chairman at an Annual Meeting how long he has known his non-executive directors, the answer 'since we were at school together' would seriously damage his credibility.

In general, the more open and consultative the appointment and selection process, the better. Sir Adrian Cadbury[4] is far from alone when he condemns the word-of-mouth, old-boy recommendation appointment route. 'Any hint of patronage undermines the quality of independence of thought, for which directors were selected in the first place.' He goes on to recommend using an impartial external agent to identify and shortlist candidates. Given the nature of one of the authors' business, it is hard for us to argue against that recommendation. However, where a company has a strong and widely respected human resources or personnel director there may well be an argument for applying much the same selection processes as for other senior management jobs—and these may or may not include external help in recruitment.

Similar issues arise over the firing of board members. If the need arises to debate the future of a main board colleague, says Gordon Owen, the independent directors should have the opportunity to do so without the chairman being present but with the person in question available. When Owen left Cable and Wireless, there was no debate at the board, it was all done on a one-to-one basis.

Should a chairman fire an independent director on his or her own? A very serious question. Should a director or independent director be asked to leave without the board as a whole voting on it? Certainly not. However, there may be a rubber stamp decision if the independent director is blatantly poor or wants to leave.

Summary

Finding the right candidate for the job cannot be left to chance or to the existing directors' own networks. Doing so reinforces current imbalances in the composition of independent director teams and loses the potential benefits of bringing on to the board people with a genuinely different perspective. Figure 6.1 gives the recommendations of the London Stock Exchange/PRO NED on selection.

A survey by the London Stock Exchange and PRO NED in 1991 and 1992 drew responses from 500 senior executives on a variety of issues concerning independent directors. Many of the recommendations by the executives concerned selection and recruitment issues. The Stock Exchange summarized these recommendations as in Figure 6.1:

- Discussions by the whole board on the qualities and contribution expected of any non-executive appointment.
- Agreement on the selection process and the formation of a representative nomination committee (only 11 per cent of companies formed a nomination committee for their last appointment).
- Preparation of a written candidate/job profile (only 23 per cent of companies had done so).
- Thorough search and preparation of a shortlist of candidates before the final selection (only 23 per cent of companies produced a shortlist).
- Letter of appointment setting down the role and proposed induction/ training programme (only 33 per cent of respondents claimed this procedure).
- Annual review by the whole board of the interaction between executive and non-executive directors, particularly the contribution to strategic debate.

Figure 6.1 The London Stock Exchange/PRO NED recommendations on selection.

References

1. *The Board and the Non-Executive Director: Improving Boardroom Performance.* The PA Consulting Group, 1991.
2. Research into the Role of the Non-Executive Director: Executive Summary. A survey jointly sponsored by PRO NED and the London Stock Exchange, PRO NED, July 1992.

3. David Clutterbuck and Marion Devine, *Businesswoman*. Macmillan, 1987.
4. Graham Searjeant, Abolish title of non-executive directors. *The Times*, 30 September 1991.

7 How to become an independent director and when to stop

At present, 99 per cent of the top 200 UK companies have at least one non-executive director. On average there are approximately four on each of the boards of *The Times* Top 1000.

Over the rest of the 1990s, the demand for high calibre independent directors will grow rapidly. The reasons are several. For a start, public pressure for more effective corporate governance will make more and more companies feel that they have to have some, in order to at least appear well managed. Whether these companies are truly prepared to use their independent directors effectively will depend to a large extent on the attitude and understanding of the chairman and chief executive.

A second reason is that, in the wake of the Cadbury Committee and other strictures against the concept that one individual can hold multiple independent directorships and properly discharge his or her duties to all of them, companies will increasingly be seeking suitable candidates who do not have several other independent director posts. They will also in many cases strengthen the independent director contingent from one or two individuals into a larger group more capable of asserting itself against the executive team.

The need to broaden the talent base provides a third reason to anticipate increasing demand for independent directors. In order to encourage equal opportunities, many large and small companies recognize the need to set an example at the top. A token female or Asian director is no longer an adequate response—companies are having to expend much greater efforts identifying individuals who have the competence to contribute significantly and to be seen to do so.

Much has been written recently about the need to recruit high calibre independent directors on to the boards of British companies. The subject of who these people should be and where they might come from has so far received considerably less attention.

We introduced this book with the statement that there are currently some 8000 non-executive directors of private sector companies in the United Kingdom, plus at least 4000 holding similar positions in public sector bodies and voluntary organizations. On a personal level, the tragedy is that the most suitable candidates are often so busy in their current executive jobs that they fail to recognize the value a non-executive directorship could add to their career development. As a result many miss out on what Sir John Harvey-Jones,[1] the former chairman of ICI, described as 'the greatest learning experience of all for a professional manager'.

A rough estimate of both public and private sector demand is that there will need to be at least 6000 new non-executive directors over the next five years.

In earlier chapters we have tried to answer a number of important questions; among them: where are these people going to come from? How are they going to gain the experience they need to take on a very different and demanding job when it is done effectively? And how can companies identify them and what will they have to do to persuade them to take up independent director positions? In essence, the answers to all these questions lie in a more professional and rigorous approach to the recruitment and induction of independent directors. This will of itself involve a widening of the pool from which candidates are drawn.

Of course, there is no shortage of people who fancy themselves as non-executive directors. The very term (you will notice that we have generally preferred 'independent directors') implies substantial status without the troublesome burden of responsibility for making things happen. We hope we have described sufficiently vividly what the position should entail, to discourage the individual who sees it as either an ego-booster or a valuable source of income, or a way to fill idle days of retirement or redundancy. Indeed, we could almost say that the more desperately someone wants an independent directorship, the less likely he or she is to have the qualities needed to do the job.

The most suitable candidates are frequently people who are so busy in their current executive jobs that they have little time to fret about non-executive jobs elsewhere. The money they might earn from an independent directorship is useful, but marginal—there are many other ways they could earn more. And, far from looking to retirement, these people are at the peak of their careers, in their forties and early fifties.

The tragedy is that so many of them will miss the opportunity to hold an independent directorship, because they do not recognize how valuable it can be to their career development. In our experience, when such individuals finally recognize the benefits of networking, of gaining different perspectives and solving different business problems, they almost universally become converts.

However, just making the decision to become an independent director is not enough. Opportunities may just fall into your lap, but unless you fit the archetypal profile (white, male, Oxbridge educated and already on the board of a major plc) do not count on it. You will need to develop a coherent approach to establishing your credentials and to opening up the right contacts.

Non-executive director positions are not retirement presents. By that time it is—or should be—too late. There are, of course, a number of well-known 'professional non-executive directors' for whom the normal rules do not apply. These include Sir John Harvey-Jones, Sir Graham Day and others whose reputations are enough to secure them a steady stream of offers.

It is possible that opportunities will fall into the laps of less well-known managers, too. But unless they fit the archetypal profile, they should not count on it. Most will need to establish their non-executive credentials and work hard to create the right contacts.

According to Barry Dinan of Hanson Green (the principal source for independent director appointments via search), for most people the best time to look for a non-executive post is when they are ten years off retirement and too busy. That is when they represent the best value to a host company for the following reasons:

- They are likely to be at the peak of their abilities, offering the best blend of experience and drive.
- They are worth developing because they can contribute to the continuity of the company.
- They have contacts who are contemporaries and, therefore, also likely to be around for the next ten years.
- They are perceived as active managers rather than serving out their time, or winding down.
- They are in demand and therefore perceived as valuable.

Those who fit this profile have much to offer a host company. They constitute excellent value for money in terms of cheap consultancy and represent an investment to help in both good and bad times. In fact, the only cloud on the horizon for suitable would-be independent directors is that there are a lot of other closet independent directors out there, too. But even this will be at least partially offset in the next few years by the increase in the number of positions on offer.

How to become an independent director

The following checklist covers the key steps in this process.

When is the right time to start?

People often leave it too late. The time to start is in the mid- to late thirties, when key career paths have begun to solidify and progress within your own company has brought you within a layer or so of a divisional board. This is the time to make your non-executive ambitions known, not least because it will normally reflect well on the scope of your personal vision (an important characteristic in the next steps of executive management).

Do not let the fact that you are also at the peak of personal input into your executive job deter you. You know the value of prioritizing and how important it is to balance short-term and long-term issues. By making an independent directorship a priority long-term objective, you can begin to focus mental energy on planning and preparation, without taking up a great deal of time.

If, on the other hand, you relegate the issue to the bottom of your priority file, you may still eventually become an independent director, but you will then most likely be in your mid- to late fifties. And, of course, you will have lost all the opportunities to feed the independent director experience back into your personal management development.

The vast majority of the respondents to our survey[2] (77 per cent) felt that the time to take an independent director position is after you reach the board of your own company. However, a substantial minority (all but one of the rest of the respondents) said the best time was before reaching the board of your own company. The arguments for each view depend on the objectives you set. If your objective is to gain experience that will enhance your capacity to achieve an executive director position, then the earlier you acquire an independent directorship, the better. If your objective is primarily to contribute to another company, and continued challenge is the main motivation, then you will best wait until you have achieved your executive board ambitions.

Why do you want to do it?

A few paragraphs ago, we examined some of the invalid reasons people want to become non-executive directors. In Chapter 3 we looked at some valid reasons. If you are going to achieve your ambition at the time it will be of most benefit to you, you must be very clear about your motivations. Typical questions you should reflect on include:

- How will this help me in my career in this company? (Will it make it easier for me to get on to the board here?)
- How will it help me in my career more generally? (Could it speed my progress to becoming chief executive elsewhere?)

- Will it make me more marketable?
- Will it broaden my skills base?
- Will it bring prestige among my peers?

The answers to these questions will also help you decide on the kind of independent directorship (role, sector, etc.) for which you should be aiming.

A word of caution here for consultants is that most boards do not want a consultant masquerading as a non-executive director. While it is true that at times the independent director role provides a cheap source of consultancy to the company, there is an important distinction between that and the role of a consultant adding one more assignment.

Define and manage a development path

Ideally, as a confident manager who has learnt how to manage yourself, you will already have at least a rough career development plan, into which your first independent directorship fits more or less comfortably. Many of the activities you undertake in pursuit of those broader personal development goals will assist you in your goal of becoming an independent director.

For example, you will need to develop networks both within and outside the company. Effective networks provide you with valuable intelligence about opportunities, warning signs to avoid dangerous political minefields, and access to people who can influence the direction and speed of your career progress. Useful networks can include the following:

- Current independent directors, who can help you understand the nature of the job and who can introduce you to interesting opportunities
- A sympathetic search company. Unfortunately many headhunters shun this role. 'Too little demand'; 'not enough demand' or 'might do it as a favour' are typical reactions. But this is short-sighted. In the future, an increasing number of firms will be willing to pay for high calibre independent directors. You can expect to have to

sell yourself and the concept to them, but it will be worth it in the long-run for the doors it can open.

- Committees of local and national bodies such as the Confederation of British Industry, Institute of Directors, Chambers of Commerce; of professional organizations, such as the Chartered Institute of Marketing, Institute of Personnel Management, Association of Corporate Treasurers, Institute of Chartered Accountants; and of trade federations, such as the Engineering Employers' Federation or the Society of Motor Manufacturers and Traders. Significantly, the independent directors in our survey considered this generally to be the equal most valuable approach, alongside headhunters.
- Consultants.
- The various independent director databases (for instance, PRO NED and Institute of Directors for the private sector).
- Training and Enterprise Councils and similar quasi-governmental organizations.

You will also want to define the skills and experience you need (see Chapter 3) and look for ways to develop them over a period of years. Having identified an area of personal development need, you can achieve a great deal through 'borrowed knowledge'—books, courses, attending conferences and so on—but the really valuable learning comes from doing. Seek opportunities to join task forces or prepare reports in these areas; perhaps even arrange a job transfer into another area if it will give you the well-rounded record you need. Obtain some exposure to overseas operations (without spending so long in the wilderness that you forget how to handle the politics back home). Above all, avoid being trapped into a narrow functional job with little opportunity to contribute beyond its boundaries.

Many successful independent directors from untypical backgrounds tend to have acquired board-type experience in other, similar but non-business situations. They may, for example, be school governors, representatives on local enterprise agencies, members of Local Health Authorities or National Health Trusts, or on the board of a national charity.

These appointments not only provide valuable experience; they also enlarge your networks. (Chairmen of plcs like to serve on national charities, in particular—not least, say cynical commentators, because they believe it helps towards a knighthood.)

An increasingly common route to extending the skills base is to continue your management education, through MBA studies and/or beyond. Choosing the right subject for your doctoral thesis can open a remarkable number of doors, both during the research and afterwards.

Such valuable activities also increase your visibility, both inside your own company and to prospective host companies. Of course, there are a lot of other ways you can raise your profile, too. Getting on the lecture circuit helps, as does appearing in print. One major consulting company now incentivizes its consultants to become 'thought-leaders'—people who develop specialist expertise and write widely about it. If your company permits, you may also be able to develop consultancy business of your own, which again brings you into contact with other companies' chairmen and directors.

In short, almost anything you do that could raise your profile internally can be adapted with little effort to raise it externally as well.

As a regular personal development exercise, we recommend that you conduct an annual or biannual SWOT (strengths, weaknesses, opportunities and threats) analysis of your progress towards an independent directorship. Set specific goals or stepping stones for the following period, in terms of extending your network, achieving particular experience, gaining specific appointments and so on.

Of course, few career plans work out exactly as intended, but that is not the point. By developing more and more options, you increase the likelihood and bring forward the time when someone asks you: 'Have you ever considered taking on a non-executive post?'

Do some homework on likely target companies

Get to know the culture of the firm. What sort of independent directors do they have now? How did they get appointed? Is the company going through major change? What competencies do you have that they would find useful at *board level*? (It is easy to assume wrongly that, just because a company needs a particular skill, it will necessarily want to build that in at board level. In reality, most requirements are for implementation skills.)

The basic sources to find out more about your target companies are:

- *The Times* Top 1000.
- The *KOMPASS Directory* which lists details from products to profits on nearly all companies in the United Kingdom.
- Annual reports, which can be obtained by writing to the company concerned.
- Company House has microfiche of each company's records since they were founded.
- Print media is a good source of up-to-date information and will post back copies of known articles. If the exact dates and journals are not known, the Textline service at the Institute of Directors will locate past articles on any given subject or company for a small fee.
- The *Crawfords Directory* gives the most recent financial analysis on most companies.

Some knowledge of the character of the chairman can also be very useful as he or she will have the last word on the appointment of independent directors. It can pay to offer him or her some appetizers such as a useful contact, or a lunch invitation that offers access to a new business forum. Of course, everyone is well aware that there is no such thing as a free lunch, but you never know where it can lead.

Be open about your ambitions

Experience indicates that some of the best candidates as independent directors lose opportunities because they fail to be overt about their ambitions. Part of the reason may be that people still often see an independent directorship as a kind of honour and, of course, being British one does not overtly push oneself forward for honours. (It is much more acceptable to contribute to political parties, sponsor the Arts and employ a public relations agency to handle the lobbying!)

Yet this very diffidence may well persuade the chairman with an independent director vacancy that you are not really interested. Once you are ready to take on an independent directorship, there is very little harm in making the fact known. If your networks are good enough, your availability and interest will become rapidly known.

If you are not sure whether you are ready to come out into the open, a specialist headhunter will often provide free and insightful guidance. He or she will also help you think through what kind of company would best be able to make use of your talents as an independent director.

Thereafter, it is only a matter of time before most suitable candidates receive an interesting offer. If you do not, you should either revisit your game plan and seek professional advice; or join a prestigious golf club!

Do look gift horses in the mouth

Some executives are so flattered, indeed relieved, when they finally receive an offer to become an independent director, that their normal caution deserts them. In some circles, there is a macho pressure to acquire independent director posts, rather like Red Indians collecting scalps, as visible evidence of management virility.

However, taking on the wrong independent directorship can be a disastrous career move. Says Colin St Johnston, managing director of PRO NED: 'Don't jump at the first offer, especially if the company is in a difficult situation. You can lose your reputation and standing very quickly in such a situation.'

St Johnston also advises would-be independent directors to research the host company thoroughly—'Once you are an independent director, you cannot walk away without a very good reason.'

Major pitfalls to look out for:

- *Basic administration details*—can you actually do the job? It has been known for people to accept independent directorships only to discover subsequently that the dates of board meetings coincide with those of their own company.
- *Chairmen who are unable or unwilling to be very precise about what is expected of you*
- *Companies, where the existing independent directors are not respected, or are not contributing.* Says Sir Anthony Gill: 'I have backed off from a couple of companies where I didn't like the combination of the challenge and the calibre of the existing independent directors—in particular where the independent directors were mainly in their seventies.'
- *Excessive demands on your time.* Reassurances that 'This won't be too demanding, I hope' all too often turn out to be hopelessly optimistic. As a basic ground rule, the more troubled the company, the more demanding it will be of the independent director's time. Companies going through major changes (rapid growth, moving into new markets or out of old ones) also tend to require more input. Family companies, where there are succession issues, may also be very demanding.
- *Being used as a Trojan Horse.* A chief executive may invite an independent director onto the board with the aim of adding an ally, who will help keep strong executives at bay. This is a no-win situation for the independent director, who risks alienating the chief executive if he or she does not openly support him, or being despised by the other executives, if he or she does.
- *Unfulfillable expectations.* The existing board members may not articulate all of their expectations. For example, they may expect the independent director to use his or her connections to secure high level introductions, or even to secure business directly. A clear contract can help avoid these problems, but the independent director should also

make sure that he or she has an opportunity to explore all the host company's motivations, both spoken and unspoken, in a formal face-to-face discussion.

- *Being the only independent director on a board.* Unless the role is primarily that of consultant/mentor, the lone independent voice can usually carry very little weight and may actually be resented for constantly questioning decisions that have already been discussed by the executives in other, operational meetings.
- *Joining a toby jug set.* Some companies have collected a coterie of independent directors, who are uniformly comfortable, well-past retirement age and of long service. They may well have appointed most of the executive team and grown protective of them. Like toby jugs, they sit on the shelf and gather dust, being there more for show than use. Apprenticeship into this club is like emigrating to a Welsh village—it takes years to be accepted. Moreover, any newcomer who champions change is likely to find both the executives and the other independents ranged in opposition.
- *Misreading the politics.* Kep Simpson candidly recounts an experience as independent chairman of a small company:

I didn't assess the persona correctly, because in this case I looked at the company more as a consultant would and failed to recognise the stark reality—it was a specialised supplier for one company where one person made the sales happen. The initial strategy to dilute this person's contribution to the point where he was not needed wasn't viable.

The former chairman, who retired shortly after I joined the board, was able to exit as a millionaire. I resigned after two years and gave back my shares, which had cost me £20,000. I was able to get something back by using the tax loss, but it was a hard and expensive lesson.

- *Being used as camouflage.* Says another non-executive director:

If you think you are being brought in as an independent director to lend pseudo-credibility to the board of a company which is a bit fast around the block, then get off it. You won't change it. I still believe—even in these days of contract smallprint—that if you shake hands on a deal it should stand. If I wasn't comfortable with the way a company operated I would resign. It's to do with a style of doing business.

- *Time*—especially when the company is in difficulty, fending off takeovers, or making frequent or major acquisitions. Says another independent chairman:

  Allocating time is always difficult. It always demands at least twice as much as you expect. If you are an independent chairman, you have to make yourself available at all times. With two or three positions of this kind, you may find that all the companies have time-consuming problems at once—so you can't afford to take on too many.

- John Heywood, a director of Clayhithe, who is a non-executive director of Ferranti, had a similarly painful experience. When the International Signals and Controls fraud was exposed, Heywood had to devote more time than he had expected and worry far more than he wanted.
- *Being expected to work miracles*. Sometimes an independent director is appointed, often as chairman, only when the company is doing badly. Once he or she is on board, institutions and colleagues relax. While their attention is elsewhere, the company fails. Examples even include Sir John Harvey-Jones as chairman of Burns Anderson, the West Country based financial services group; and Sir Ian McGregor of British Coal fame. When McGregor joined Hunter Print and Mountleigh, they thought he could walk on water, but both companies failed.

  When faced with a troubled company, the newly appointed independent director must ensure first and foremost that the commitment of everyone—investors, board colleagues and executive management—is firm.

The same independent chairman is in demand as a company doctor. In choosing whether to accept an independent director position on a troubled company's board, he takes a number of factors into account:

- Has it the *written* support of investors and bankers for at least three to six months?
- What resources are there in the company, in terms of people, management, market potential and so on?
- Is the finance director someone of the appropriate calibre?

He also insists on seeing the main lender of money—partly for reassurance, partly because 'It's a contest to some extent, who becomes chairman.'

The main task of a chairman in these circumstances, he believes is 'to get everyone moving in the same direction'.

Many of these pitfalls can be avoided by seeking professional advice before making any commitments. It also helps if the post is being filled through the offices of a headhunter—who should be experienced enough in the likely problems to have raised the relevant questions with the company at the specification stage.

However, it would be a shame to end the main part of this book on such a negative note. With careful forethought and a refusal to be rushed into a decision, the would-be independent director will easily avoid most of these problems: to be forewarned is to be forearmed.

The truth is that many independent directors do establish excellent working relationships with their executive and non-executive colleagues on British company boards. Both they and the companies benefit from the arrangement, and so do the shareholders. The key is for the arrangement to be managed on both sides in a thoroughly professional manner. Clearly, too, one of the most important talents of an effective independent director is knowing when to quit. That is why we have devoted the last section of this chapter to the question of when an independent director should resign, either to make way for fresh ideas or to maintain the integrity of the non-executive role.

WHEN THE INDEPENDENT DIRECTOR SHOULD RESIGN

Our survey shows that there is broad consensus among independent directors about a number of issues that constitute cause for resignation. When asked what would cause them to quit:

- 94 per cent said reservations about the ethical behaviour of the top team.
- 89 per cent said they would not stay if there was a conflict of interest.
- 86 per cent said they would go if key information was being withheld.
- 81 per cent said they would quit over a major policy disagreement.

Other issues, however, are more subjective. For example, only 39 per cent said they would resign if they had a personality clash with chairman or chief executive.

Interestingly, too, only 19 per cent said that they had ever actually resigned for the reasons discussed.

We believe that, essentially, an independent director should be prepared to resign whenever he or she fundamentally disagrees with the company's actions or policies and cannot bring about the changes he or she believes necessary. The independent director has an obligation at least to try to make change happen, by exhortation, persuasion and, where practical, bringing in external advice and pressure (e.g. from investors).

The difficulties lie firstly in deciding what is a fundamental disagreement and secondly in knowing what is actually going on. Examples of fundamental disagreements might include:

- Unwise investments or acquisitions.
- The 'wrong' marketing strategy.
- Immoral or illegal behaviour on the part of executives who cannot be removed from their post. (In the latter case, the independent director may have an obligation to take the matter up with the auditors, the investment

institutions, a professional body, or, in extremis, the police.)

In the event of dishonest activities involving the chairman of a company, for example, independent directors have a unique opportunity and a legitimate responsibility to ask the questions that others will not ask.

Says David O'Shaugnessy: 'If all attempts to bring pressure to bear are unsuccessful, including attempts to involve the company's professional advisers—the bankers, lawyers, auditors, etc.—then resignation with maximum publicity is the independent director's last recourse.' Such situations can be highly stressful and complex.

Recalls one independent director: 'I was chairman of the remuneration committee of a public sector organization. It was quite clear what had to be done, but I found myself in constant conflict with the Treasury. In the end, I decided that the only course open to me was to resign as a public gesture to the Government, who were the shareholders.' At least part of this director's motivation was to avoid the possibility of all the independent directors feeling they had to resign.

Kep Simpson recalls a situation where he felt obliged to quit:

> With one company I was invited to join as an independent director, I soon found myself so out of sympathy with the executive directors that we terminated the arrangement after a year. They wanted to position themselves for sale to a larger group and didn't really want any distractions. However, I did persuade them to sell their head office at the height of the property market and before the property crash.

Dr Brian Smith feels it would be appropriate to resign: 'if I was isolated in a view that I held very strongly on a fundamental issue. It might be the direction the company was taking. Or it could be the manner in which it was intending to go about its strategy such as borrowing a large amount of money.'

Pat Rich, chairman and chief executive of BOC, faced an interesting dilemma when he joined the board of a management institution. 'I resigned', he explains, 'because I felt their own corporate governance was inadequate when they were purporting to teach other companies about corporate governance. I didn't believe that one board meeting with 60 people every six months was enough.'

A specific situation where independent directors should consider quitting is when a new chairman is appointed—particularly in circumstances where the company is in deteriorating financial health. Says company doctor Clive Bastin: 'Sometimes I find all the independent directors offer their resignation to the incoming chairman as a matter of good practice.' Equally, this same director is not slow to demand the resignation of independent directors 'if they have been part of the problem and have not blown the whistle on poor management'.

SUMMARY

It is not who you know that counts in becoming an independent director, but who knows you. The nature and quality of networks is critical. Acquiring the right level and kind of experience is a major success factor (see Figure 7.1), as is a willingness to make yourself known as a potential candidate.

IN CONCLUSION

Much of this book has necessarily been negative. Misconceptions and past subversions of the role of the non-executive or independent director required us to take a critical view. However, we are optimistic—bullish even—about the future.

The good news for British companies and would-be independent directors alike, is that our research indicates a move towards a reassessment of the non-executive role in this country. The signal failure of existing corporate governance arrangements to prevent the misuse of executive power in a number of recent cases and the recommendations of the Cadbury Committee, will give added momentum to this trend.

As more and more companies recognize the value that objectively selected independent directors can add to their businesses, and as the career development benefits and opportunities become more widely understood, so the potential of the non-executive director role will increasingly be fulfilled. This in turn will lead to an inevitable reshuffling of the executive pack which will be good for British companies, and good for United Kingdom plc.

Marks and Spencer, National Grid and BASF are among 100 companies participating in Annex which is effectively a nursery for non-executive directors originated by one of the authors and proving increasingly successful. The benefits Annex provides for participants include:

- Board-level involvement in other companies and sectors makes candidate independent directors realize there is no such thing as a unique business problem—there is always someone, somewhere who has faced something similar.
- High-flyers with itchy feet realize that the grass is no greener elsewhere—which helps retention.
- Candidate independent directors gain experience of the real thing, not just playing at business games. There is a real job to be done on the board of the host company.
- It helps to motivate key people by exposing them to a different culture outside their own firm.
- It brings together the very brightest from two companies and from different business cultures, enabling them to meet at an early stage in their careers. As they gain promotion they can keep in touch and continue to expand their networks.
- Appointments need not be on to main boards, but can include the boards of subsidiary companies. While the experience at this level may not at first sight seem particularly valuable if the subsidiary board is a board only in name and meets infrequently, affiliation to more than one subsidiary board in the same group can provide a good portfolio. The candidate independent director could also become a member of a task force or executive committee or even PA to the chairman. (The advantage of not being a 'real' board is that the non-executive director is not a 'real' director and therefore has the chance to feel out the director role without the burden of legal responsibilities associated with a directorship.)
- It meets the need to get out of the candidate's existing business culture, especially in cases where the company has a reputation for home-growing its talent.
- The candidate 'comes of age', knows himself or herself, in a way not unlike an extended outward bound course.

- While not a substitute for training, non-executive roles supplement it offering experience as a director.
- It helps women get crucial experience at director level.
- It helps the donor company retain key staff, especially after a major reorganization when it is important to motivate those who stay behind and make them feel wanted.
- Since most companies know who their bright prospects are—they probably do not have that many of them—independent director posts offer a staging post that allows individuals to feel they are being groomed for the home board.
- For the receiving, or host board, it offers an external yardstick. Competitors are always moving and incoming high-flyers from other companies help the host company to question its own standards and to avoid inertia in its management thinking.
- Occasionally a candidate independent director may find that the grass really is greener elsewhere. In such cases it is best for the donor company to realize that the individual is unsettled before it invests more time and money in grooming him or her for the executive director role.

One independent director-hopeful under the Annex scheme is 41-year-old Hugh Reader, general manager of information technology at WH Smith. Reader sees a non-executive position as an opportunity to broaden his business knowledge. 'I'm not looking to get involved as an I.T. specialist,' he says, 'I'm more interested in learning from experience outside of my own corporate culture.'

Figure 7.1 The Annex Scheme. © Copyright Hanson Green.

REFERENCES

1. Sir John Harvey-Jones, *Making it Happen: Reflections on Leadership*. Collins, 1988.
2. Making the most of Non-Executive Directors—a survey by Hanson Green and The ITEM Group plc, 1992.

Appendix 1
More legal background

An individual may be disqualified from being a director:

1. On conviction of an indictable offence in connection with company business.
2. For persistent breaches of company's legislation.
3. For fraud in the course of the winding up of a company.
4. On conviction for a summary offence for failing to comply with the provisions of the company's legislation requiring, for example, filing of returns or accounts, etc.
5. If, as a director of an insolvent company, the court is satisfied that an individual's conduct as a director makes him/her unfit to be concerned in the company's management.

CIVIL LIABILITY

Directors may find themselves involved in civil litigation for breach of *due care* requirements. These require directors to exercise reasonable care in pursuance of their duties.

Litigation over due care is most common in the United States, where case law has set a number of precedents. The key question considered by the courts is 'what would a reasonable, careful person have done in the circumstances?' There is an assumption that directors have acted in good faith in the interests of the company unless it can be proven otherwise. There is also an assumption that boards can approve reasonable risks, on the basis that there are few gains without some risks, and that directors do not guarantee that their actions will result in profits.

However, a number of directors of major US corporations

have found themselves at the losing end of shareholder suits. In one case, a board approved a merger with another company, based on price and commercial information supplied by one of its members. The decision was subsequently contested under due care provision and the board members were held by the court to have been negligent. The reasoning behind the judgment was that:

- the decision was taken at a meeting where the issue was not on the agenda
- the only information was a 20-minute presentation by the proposing director
- the decision was taken in only two hours.

In another case, the courts found that the opinion of a financial expert on a major investment was not discussed. Again, this was held to be a breach of due care.

US companies have, not surprisingly, tended in recent years to tighten up boardroom procedures. In particular, they take more detailed minutes, as a source of documentary proof of the extent and depth of discussion of important decisions. Practice in the UK may well follow suit.

INSIDER DEALING

The basic principle of insider dealing is one of equality of information—everyone in the market must have equal access to information about the company. Those entrusted with confidential information must not use it to gain personal advantage or communicate to others who may do so. The penalties in most developed countries (including, Germany, which had until recently a very lax approach to insider dealing) involve imprisonment and severe fines.

Confidential information can be defined as 'information which, if it were published, would influence the price/share'. A deal concluded with insider information is invalid. Any third party, who can demonstrate a loss from insider trading, may seek damages from the perpetrators.

For a more detailed review of the legislation affecting directors, see *Directors: Duties and Liabilities* (Feb. 1993) commissioned by Hanson Green and published by City solicitors Freshfields.

Appendix 2
A recommended letter of engagement

In his book, *Non-Executive Directors*, Ken Lindon-Travers[1] suggests a number of points that should be covered. The following engagement letter is a composite drawn up by us to incorporate his main points and is supplemented by our direct experience.

TERMS AND CONDITIONS OF ENGAGEMENT

Your appointment will be that of ....

Your appointment will commence on .... and will be for an initial period of one year, renewable, and reviewed annually between .... and yourself.

As non-executive chairman/director, you will be an independent member of the main board and will not have a contractual connection with .... other than the office of non-executive chairman/director, or any involvement with the company, its directors or management which could affect the exercise of independent judgement.

Neither will you have a relationship, which may stem from prior executive responsibilities, association with the company's professional advisers, or the representation of financial institutions, major shareholders or various sectional interests.

It is agreed that you have or will have always notified .... in all areas where conflict of interests may arise.

You, as non-executive chairman/director, will accept the legal responsibility to act bona fide, with due diligence and care, in the interests of .... as a whole and in parity with executive directors. (The 'interests of ....' embraces its relationship with and the interests of all employees, suppliers, customers and shareholders.)

................acknowledges your common law right of access to information needed to perform your duties.

An appropriate annual time commitment will be .... at a rate of .... per annum subject to review. All reasonable expenses incurred on behalf of .... will be reimbursed. These financial arrangements fully take into account the nature and scope of the non-executive chairman's/director's anticipated contribution.

You, as a non-executive chairman/director, have a right to resign if you feel the main board persists in a course of action which is believed to be contrary to the interests of .... Termination of service as non-executive chairman/director may be given at any time, by either party, without implied compensation.

I would appreciate it if you could sign below and return one copy to .... for our retention.

I, ... agree to these terms and conditions as outlined in your statement dated ....

Signed ....
Date ....

Since this letter is, of necessity, formal and legalistic, a friendly covering letter should also accompany it.

REFERENCES

1. Ken Lindon-Travers, *Non-Executive Directors*, Director Books, 1990.

Appendix 3
The survey

In writing this book we drew heavily on the personal experiences of both the people who were willing to talk to us—on and off the record—and our own backgrounds. As authors we were fortunate to be able to bring to bear the methodology of an experienced management journalist and consultant and the experience of a full-time non-executive search consultant.

To gather the background information that would give us insight into the practicalities of the independent director role, we also carried out a detailed survey, to which 38 independent directors responded. In addition, we carried out numerous in-person and telephone interviews, both structured and unstructured, to gather data on specific aspects of the independent director role.

The survey questionnaire is reproduced on pages 211–219. It contains three main themes:

- The broad scope of their activities as independent directors.
- Details of up to three of their current appointments.
- Their opinions on some of the key issues.

THE BROAD SCOPE OF THEIR ACTIVITIES

The independent directors held on average 2.7 positions with 37 per cent holding both private and public posts. Private sector appointments (highest number seven) outnumbered public sector (highest number four). Views differed considerably on how many independent director positions one person could handle effectively, ranging from two to twelve. Many of the respondents drew a distinction between the individual, who currently has executive responsibilities (who they most commonly considered should have no more than two or three posts) and the manager who holds no executive responsibilities.

The majority of respondents (68 per cent) considered that independent directors *should* normally have current executive posts, although they were equally (and more) of the opinion that independent directors *can* still be very effective members of the board if they do not. There was also a strong feeling (76 per cent) that independent directors should not be from the same industry sector or background. Yet at the same time, just under half considered that a different industry sector or background was not necessary. The apparent contradiction is explained by comments such as: 'a balance is needed,' or 'an experience in retailing in one industry sector could be a useful background to a company with retail interests in another sector... an independent director must be able to contribute to the operations of a company by virtue of experience'.

By and large, independent directors welcomed the opportunity to assist troubled companies, as long as there was some chance of a turnaround. Among the reasons they gave: 'The chance to contribute to change and progress,' 'an independent director could make a significant contribution,' 'challenge and opportunity,' 'independent directors who want the dolce vita are useless!' 'my experience could help those in trouble,' 'happy to do so if there is a prospect of a turnaround,' 'success [in turnaround] is very rewarding,' 'the challenge of contributing new/different perspectives,' 'the satisfaction and opportunity to be of value are greater,' 'more opportunity for input—companies in trouble are more likely to seek advice and guidance,' 'opportunity to learn,' 'the challenge and financial reward,' 'the challenge and the total involvement that occurs during such a period'.

However, a significant minority would avoid serving on troubled companies, on the grounds that: 'as a busy executive it would probably be too demanding on time,' 'an independent director has legal responsibility without executive authority,' 'because my expertise is not in the financial area', 'too time consuming'.

Virtually none of the independent directors had had any training in the special requirements of the non-executive role. Such training as they had received amounted to 'running a plc' rather than specific development activity. By contrast, just over two-thirds of replies had had training in executive direction.

THEIR CURRENT APPOINTMENTS

Most appointments of independent directors were made as a result of a direct approach by the CEO or by someone else in the organization (the chairman or, in one case, a major shareholder). Less than 20 per cent were approached by headhunters and about 14 per cent of contacts were initiated by the independent director himself or herself. Some public appointments came about because the individual's name was on a list. In practice, appointments came about in many cases from contacts at several levels and in several ways, presumably over a period.

In about one-third of cases, respondents considered that the method of appointment enhanced their status; in two-thirds of instances, respondents said it made no difference to their status. In only two cases was it a negative factor.

The tenure of appointments tends to be relatively long compared with, say, consultants. Approximately 40 per cent of the main appointments had been in place for three years or more and the same proportion for between one and three years.

Asked how much they knew about the company beforehand, the independent directors tended equally to 'very little' and 'quite a lot'. Very few knew a great deal about the company, but 17 per cent knew nothing at all about it.

Those that did have a knowledge of the company frequently gained it through press reports (23 per cent). Other common methods were as a friend of one of the directors (13 per cent) and from working in the company as an executive or senior manager (6 per cent). Among other routes were working for the company as a consultant or as the external legal adviser, or as former auditors; personal research; from government briefings; contact with an associate organization; as a shareholder; as a sponsor of the company's buyout; 'from reliable analysts'; and via a trade association.

Although in most cases the role the independent director was expected to play was defined clearly, this was not the case 27 per cent of the time. Where the role was clearly defined, 15 per cent of independent directors had to provide the definition themselves. Slightly more (21 per cent) had it defined for them by outside parties such as an investment bank, City advisers or the Government.

Half of the independent directors received a clear contract. Of those who did, all had their salary spelt out, but only just over half of these had a clear definition of roles and responsibilities or length of appointment, and only 42 per cent of the contracts specified period of notice. This suggests that normal professional practice in making appointments is not widespread for independent directors.

The independent directors believe they usually bring more than one element of expertize or background that makes them suitable for the posts they hold. The most important factor is experience at a high level of management, followed by functional expertize and by industry background.

The reasons they accepted the position also varied, with independent directors often having a mixture of motivations. The most common attractions were either altruistic (opportunity to make a contribution) or for personal development (opportunity to learn), followed by challenge. Money came way down the list—although experience by the authors suggests it may play a larger role during initial negotiation between independent director candidates and the company.

Most respondents took up their appointments within the first three months of being approached, but a significant minority (13 per cent) took up to six months. Their induction generally included briefing meetings with the chairman, but only two-thirds received written materials about the company and only just over half had meetings with other directors before taking on the responsibilities. Slightly more than one-third made site visits; only 28 per cent received previous board minutes. Very few spent time with employees at levels below the board to learn about the company. None had attended the company's normal induction programme. On the other hand, only four respondents said they had not received any form of induction at all from a company.

Although best practice might suggest that independent directors were automatically members of audit or executive remuneration committees, in fact, only 43 per cent are. Other committees attended include pensions, property, chairman's, lending policy (for a building society), planning, marketing, investment and corporate banking committees.

Most of the value independent directors bring seems to lie in the board discussions, with 83 per cent helping by challenging the assumptions of executive management and 69 per cent by bringing specialist functional knowledge. Almost half act as a mentor or confidant(e) to the chairman. About one-third provide useful business introductions and 50 per cent help select key people.

Asked about the pleasures and frustrations of being an independent director, respondents provided a wide range of reactions. Among the pleasures:

- Helping drive a new enterprise forward.
- Working with people I respect and know already.
- Policy-making without line responsibility.
- Helping to improve the performance of the board and hence the company.
- Making a contribution/feeling one is contributing constructively.
- Developing strategy and insights into a different industry.
- Learning how other businesses function (from someone holding nine independent director positions!)
- Seeing proposals put into action.
- New areas of activity and interest.
- Sense of doing one's duty.
- Independence: the ability to influence.
- Enhanced business knowledge.
- Building personal relationships.
- Involvement in new ... business problems.

By contrast, the frustrations include:

- Lack of detailed information on day-to-day activities.
- Lack of time to really get to know the companies and their people.
- Timescales to effect change.
- Corporate governance.
- Failure to make a profit worldwide.
- 'Difficulty in making a maximum contribution—for example, in contributing to strategies, in qualifying or stopping wrong decisions, all through ignorance of detailed considerations and lack of opportunity to debate, discuss or brainstorm.'
- Insufficient involvement.
- Poor information and defensive executives.
- 'High demand on time for very little remuneration, i.e. to make a contribution it is necessary to meet and discuss rising issues outside the normal board meeting timetable.'
- Not being hands-on in certain situations.
- Seeing good advice not acted upon!
- Difficulties in agreeing appointments with senior managers.
- 'Sometimes I feel better use could be made of my time!'
- Finding enough time to spend a few hours a month with the general managers of the company.
- Sometimes being bypassed in the decision-making process by the exigencies of the moment.
- Not having sufficient discussion on strategy.
- Poor presentation of material to independent directors for discussion.
- Learning about and understanding the technicalities of a business, which is very unfamiliar to me.
- Pinning down the executive directors to give clear answers.

Several respondents said there were no frustrations, although one qualified the statement by adding 'once the rationale for my appointment (to keep the peace if war broke out between the voting joint venture partners) was clear'.

Only one respondent had encountered any problems of

conflict of interest, which he had resolved 'by careful discussion'. Further study would be needed to confirm whether conflicts of interest are indeed rare.

In spite of some frustrations at the inadequacy of information presented to them, most independent directors (91 per cent) consider that they have sufficient information to make informed decisions at board meetings. However, 41 per cent hold pre-board meetings to bring independent directors up to speed on the issues to be discussed.

Most independent directors regularly receive from the companies they serve financial reports and copies of the business strategy and plan. Changes of senior personnel are usually also reported. But major gains and losses of business are reported to independent directors in only two-thirds of companies and two in five do not even send their independent directors a copy of the employee newspaper! One in three informs independent directors about quality and customer care measurements.

Contrary to some speculation, the perks of being an independent director appear to be relatively few. Only 6 per cent receive perks such as company cars or chauffeurs; 11 per cent share options; and 7 per cent a company-paid medical. Less than half receive directors' liability insurance. While they may already be insured in their own company, we suspect that for some independent directors the reason is simply a failure to appreciate the risks they run.

THE COMPANIES

The organizations covered in the survey were a mixture of public sector, private sector quoted and private sector unquoted companies. Just over two-fifths were small and medium-sized (under £50 million turnover).

INDEPENDENT DIRECTORS' OPINIONS

The independent directors in our survey differ in their views on the need for specific training for the role, with the majority coming down against, by 58 per cent to 42 per cent. Of those that do support the idea of training, the majority prefer informal courses, with some 15 per cent favouring a formal course leading to a qualification, 20 per cent preferring some form of shadowing or mentoring and 20 per cent some form of non-voting apprenticeship or observation at board meetings. Given the small numbers behind these percentages, they can only be used as rough indicators.

Opinion was also divided as to how long an independent director should hold his or her position. Just over one-third of those who answered this question felt there should be no fixed term; slightly more were in favour of a fixed term specified by contract and 16 per cent felt a maximum number of years was appropriate (suggestions varied from three to ten years). Some of those preferring no fixed term qualified their view with comments such as 'subject to periodic review by chairman and nominating committee'.

There was similar diversity of opinion over the composition of the board, with about half in favour of a majority of executives and the rest either in favour of mostly independent directors (17 per cent of those with a specific preference) or equal proportions (26 per cent). In practice, as several respondents pointed out, the issue is more complex. Comments include:

- It depends entirely on the nature of the business of the company.
- It depends on the size of the company and the experience of the executive board.
- Generalizations are dangerous. Each case is different.
- Neither segment should feel oppressed by numbers.
- There should be a two-to-one ratio in favour of independent directors; this preserves independence and separates 'governance' from 'management'.
- The balance of power must favour non-executives of true independence.
- Too many non-executives stifle innovation; too many executives and they ignore the non-executives.
- There should be a full-time executive chairman with a casting vote.

- (Mostly independent directors): it reduces the chairman's power.
- Too many independent directors would result in too many theoretical discussions.
- An independent director should be there to disturb and challenge—too many would be *too* disturbing.
- Executives must have the final say.
- (Mostly executives—but nearly equal): the various functions should be represented, but the board should not be too big.
- (Equal proportions): gives a balance of interest and argument.
- The executives run the company. If the relationship between them and the non-executives is right then a minority of non-executives is OK.
- (Mostly executives): the board controls the destiny of the company. This should not be in the hands of those who are unaccountable to employees (or shareholders).
- (Mostly executives): proper management cannot be left to part-time directors.
- (Mostly independent directors): to counter bureaucracy.
- (Mostly independent directors): to bring experience and views on good governance.
- (Mostly executives): companies need 'doers' not 'talkers' or 'advisors' in the majority.

and finally . . .

- 'Personal experience!'

From the length of the list of frustrations earlier, it is perhaps not surprising that 24 per cent of respondents consider that companies do not make as much use of their independent directors as they should. 'Look at the major collapses!' comments one.

By the same token, more than twice as many respondents consider that companies do not put sufficient effort into selecting the right independent directors, as consider they do. Respondents were, however, generally reluctant to comment on whether specific sectors were well or badly served by their independent directors.

When it comes to how independent directors can go about finding suitable posts, the equally most valuable sources were seen as membership of committees of national bodies and headhunters. These were also the most useful routes for them as individuals. 'Acting as a consultant to the company' and 'political connections' were also perceived as valuable routes.

Respondents had strong opinions on the difficulties in recruiting suitable female independent directors. The main reason suggested was simple lack of suitable candidates, but one-quarter pointed to inadequate searching procedures and one-quarter to lack of genuine commitment to using female independent directors.

Opinion was divided over whether the chairman of a large company would have difficulty adapting to the requirements of being an independent director in a small company, or vice versa. The majority (58 per cent) concluded they would not.

A sharper division occurred on the issue of whether the chairman should be executive or non-executive, with two-thirds of those who had a preference being in favour of the chairman being independent. Comments included:

- I prefer a non-executive chairman because the combination of chairman, chief executive and in many cases chief operating officer in one person is bad for the company.
- I do not think a chairman can be truly non-executive. It depends on whether there are other effective ways of ensuring correct accountability and integrity—such as a majority of independent directors.
- The chairman cannot do his job properly unless he is executive.
- 'Non-executive' is often used in place of 'part-time'.
- Either will work.
- It depends on the size and complexity of the company. The bigger it is the more the need to have a non-executive chairman.
- Non-executive probably implies semi-executive. He must be able to stand back and assess the performance of the executive directors and make the changes necessary.
- There is no general right answer.

- Preferably non-executive as the chairman should be objective and mildly detached.
- (Non-executive): should be one stage removed from the management team.
- (Executive): that is where the buck stops.
- The ideal is a chief executive and a non-executive chairman.
- (Non-executive): as a non-executive he can hold the balance.
- (Non-executive): detachment from general management is essential for balance and challenge to executives.
- This depends on the company and the chairman.
- Depends on the personality.
- It does not matter provided there is a CEO.
- Depends on size and other factors.
- Probably a hybrid is best here; but the CEO needs to be in charge of the company once the direction is agreed.

Stronger agreement (89 per cent of respondents) was registered for splitting the positions of chairman and chief executive.

The issue of when the independent director should quit also gave rise to a high degree of consensus, with approximately 84 per cent of respondents agreeing that they would feel obliged to do so if faced with situations where key information is withheld from them, or there was a conflict of interest, or they had reservations about the ethical behaviour of the executive team. Slightly fewer would resign over a major policy agreement and less than one-quarter over a personality clash with the chairman or chief executive.

The last-but-one issue related to the extent to which independent directors should get to know people just below the board. Approximately 29 per cent felt they should do so closely; 68 per cent that they should at least recognize who these people are and what they do.

Finally, we asked at what point in their career people should take their first independent directorship. The respondents came down strongly (74 per cent) in favour of once the individual has reached the board of his or her own company. This view, we suspect, reflects their own experience. None of the respondents felt that it was appropriate to gain first experience as an independent director after retirement.

MAKING THE MOST OF NON-EXECUTIVE DIRECTORS

A survey by Hanson Green and The ITEM Group plc

Please tick all appropriate answers.

A. THE BROAD SCOPE OF YOUR ACTIVITIES AS AN INDEPENDENT DIRECTOR

1. How many independent director posts do you hold?
    - in the private sector
    - in the public sector
2. What is the maximum number of independent director posts you think any individual should hold?
3. Do you currently hold any executive director posts? yes/ no?
4. With which of the following statements do you agree?
    - an independent director should normally hold a current executive post
    - an independent director can be very effective without holding any current executive posts
    - an independent director should normally be from the same general industry sector or background
    - an independent director should normally be from a different industry sector or background.
5. Would you tend to avoid or welcome the opportunity to be an independent director of a financially troubled company, as long as there were some prospect of turn-around?
    - welcome
    - avoid

    Can you briefly explain your reasons?

6. Have you ever had any specific training to be an effective non-executive director?
   - yes
   - no

   If yes, what form did it take?

7. Have you had formal training in effective *executive* direction?
   - yes
   - no

B. YOUR CURRENT APPOINTMENT

In this section we have tried to cater both for the person with one independent director position and the person with many. If you have numerous independent director posts, please choose up to three, about which you are happy to respond.

1. How were you appointed as an independent director?

                                              Co.1   Co.2   Co.3
   - you approached the company
   - you were approached directly
     by the CEO?
   - you were approached by
     someone else in the
     organization (please specify)
   - you were approached by a
     headhunter
   - your name was on a list

   Do you consider that the method of appointment enhanced or downgraded the status of the position?
   - enhanced
   - downgraded
   - made no difference

2. How long have you held this appointment?
   - less than one year
   - 1–3 years
   - more than three years

3. How much did you know about the company before-hand?

- nothing
- very little
- quite a lot
- a great deal

4. Where did you gain your prior knowledge of the company?
   - from press reports
   - as a friend of one of the directors
   - as a customer
   - as a supplier
   - as a consultant to the company
   - from working in the company as an executive or senior manager
   - other (please specify)

5. Was the role you were expected to play clearly defined?
   - yes
   - no

   If yes, who by?
   - you
   - the company
   - an outside party (please specify)

6. What elements of your expertise or background made you suitable for the position?
   - functional expertise (e.g. marketing)
   - industry background
   - experience at a particular level of management
   - knowledge of the company
   - just being part of the network
   - other (please specify)

7. What made you accept the position?
   (Please rank in order of importance.)
   - money
   - challenge
   - friendship
   - status
   - developing your networks
   - opportunity to make a contribution
   - opportunity to learn
   - other (please specify)

8. Did you receive a clear contract?
    ● yes
    ● no
    If yes, which of the following did it contain?
    ● salary
    ● roles and responsibilities
    ● length of appointment
    ● period of notice
    ● other (please specify)
9. How much time passed between when you were first approached and when you took up the appointment?
    ● less than one month
    ● 1–3 months
    ● 4–6 months
    ● more than 6 months
10. What form of induction did you undergo?
    ● meeting with the chairman/CEO
    ● meetings with other directors
    ● meetings with representative employees at all levels
    ● written materials about the company
    ● previous board minutes
    ● site visits
    ● attendance at the formal induction and orientation programme that normal employees would attend (or a version of it)
    ● none
    ● other (please specify)
11. On which of the following committees do you sit?
    ● audit
    ● remuneration
    ● ethics
    ● other (please specify)
12. What specific help have you been able to give the company?
    ● specialist knowledge in a functional area
    ● introductions to business contacts
    ● challenge assumptions by executive management
    ● selection of key personnel
    ● government relations

- act as confidant(e)/mentor to the chairman/CEO
- other (please specify)

13. What have you found to be the chief frustrations of being a non-executive director?

If you have any useful anecdotes, which would illustrate any of these points, and which you would be willing to share, please include on a separate sheet or tick the box below and complete the name and address spaces at the end. In the latter case, our researchers will contact you to talk through the anecdote(s).

14. What have you found to be the chief pleasures of being an independent director?

Again, anecdotes would be valuable.

15. Have you ever encountered any conflicts of interest in your role as an independent director? (E.g. on salary, terms and conditions, inside knowledge, competitive information.)
- yes
- no

If yes, how did you resolve them?

16. (a) Do you receive sufficient information from the company to make really informed judgements about issues raised at board meetings?
- yes
- no

(b) Does the company hold pre-board meetings, to brief independent directors on key issues before the board meeting proper?
- yes
- no

17. What information do you receive regularly from the company?
    - financial reports
    - quality and customer care measurements
    - changes of senior personnel
    - major gains and losses of business
    - the business strategy
    - the business plan
    - the company newspaper
    - compilation of press comment
    - other (please specify)

18. Does the company provide you with any of the following? (Please ignore any elements you do not wish to answer.)
    - major perks (e.g. car/chauffeur)
    - director's liability insurance
    - key man insurance
    - share options
    - company medical
    - other significant benefits
      (please specify)

C. THE COMPANY(IES) FOR WHICH YOU ARE A NON-EXECUTIVE DIRECTOR

	Co.1	Co.2	Co.3
Sector: public sector			
private sector quoted			
private sector unquoted			
Size: under £50 million			
over £50 million			

D. YOUR OPINIONS

1. Do you think independent directors should receive specific training?
   - yes
   - no
   If yes, what form should it take?

- a formal course leading to a qualification
- informal courses
- shadowing of/mentoring by an experienced independent director
- some form of non-voting apprenticeship or observation at board meetings
- other (please specify)

2. How long do you consider you should typically hold an independent director position?
   - indefinitely
   - for a period specified by contract
   - for a maximum number of years (please specify)
   - no fixed period

3. What split do you think there should be between executives and non-executives on a board?
   - mostly executives
   - mostly independent directors
   - equal proportions
   - it doesn't matter

   Do you have a specific reason for this opinion?

4. On the whole, do you consider that companies make as much use of their independent directors as they should?
   - yes
   - no

   Why?

5. Do you think companies put sufficient effort into selecting the right independent directors?

6. Do you perceive that any sectors are particularly well or badly served by independent directors? (Please specify, with reasons if you wish.)

7. What of the following do you consider to be valuable approaches to gaining independent director positions? Which have been very useful for you?

	Consider valuable	Useful for you
• membership of committees of national bodies, such as the CBI, Institute of Directors, Engineering Employers' Federation		

	Consider valuable	Useful for you
• as a consultant		
• political connections		
• public relations		
• headhunters		
• other (please specify)		

8. Why do you think it is that so many companies report difficulties in identifying suitable female independent directors?
    - inadequate searching procedures
    - simple lack of suitable candidates
    - lack of genuine commitment to using female independent directors
    - other (please specify)

9. Do you consider that an executive from a large company may have difficulty adapting to the requirements as an independent director of a small company, or vice versa?
    - yes
    - no

    Any particular reason you would like to share?

10. Should the chairman be executive or non-executive?
    - executive
    - non-executive

    Why?

11. Should the positions of chairman and chief executive be split?
    - yes
    - no

12. When would you feel obliged to quit? And have you ever done so?

	Reason to quit	Done so
• major policy disagreement		
• key information is being withheld		
• personality clash with the chairman or CEO		
• reservations about ethical behaviour of the top team		
• conflict of interest		
• other (please specify)		

13. To what extent do you believe an independent director should get to know people in the layer below the board?
    - closely
    - sufficient to recognize who they are and what they do
    - no need to know them at all
14. At what point in their career do you consider people should take their first independent director position?
    - before they reach the board of their own company
    - after they reach the board of their own company
    - after they retire
    - other (please specify)

Index